Praise for *Th*

"Boy, do we need this book now! Fr. James Mallon has given us an uplifting message for today—a book full of encouragement, resourcefulness, and hope. Drawing on Scripture, prayer, and his own life, Fr. Mallon has written an engaging work that will touch countless lives and give readers the tools to face the future with faith restored and, yes, thriving."
—Deacon Greg Kandra, blogger and author, *The Busy Person's Guide to an Extraordinary Life*

"Fr. Mallon has perfected the art of teaching through story, such that he would make the Greatest of Rabbis proud! Each chapter, an entertaining parable of personal experience mixed with key Scriptures, so captivated me that I didn't realize I was learning profound truths of the faith. A fresh invitation to be transformed through the power of God, *Thriving Faith: Discipleship in Uncertain Times* ignites a passion in all to be attentive hearers and eager doers of the Word—no matter what the world throws at you! The perfect guide for any disciple of Jesus!"
—Kelly Wahlquist, founder of WINE: Women In the New Evangelization, Director of the Archbishop Flynn Catechetical Institute in the Archdiocese of Saint Paul and Minneapolis, and author of *Created to Relate: God's Design for Peace and Joy*.

Thriving Faith

DISCIPLESHIP IN UNCERTAIN TIMES

FR. JAMES MALLON

Published by The Word Among Us Press
7115 Guilford Drive, Suite 100
Frederick, Maryland 21704
wau.org

26 25 24 23 22   1 2 3 4 5

ISBN: 978-1-59325-608-1
eISBN: 978-1-59325-609-8

Nihil obstat: The Reverend Michael Morgan, J.D., J.C.L.
Censor Librorum
June 16, 2022
Imprimatur: +Most Reverend Felipe J. Estévez, S.T.D.
June 17, 2022

Cover design by Suzanne Earl

Library of Congress Control Number: 2022910421

Contents

Introduction

Uncertainty is an accurate word to describe the times we inhabit. Throughout most of the world, the restrictions of the Covid-19 pandemic have been all but lifted, and we are learning what it means to live with the Covid-19 virus, which means living with uncertainty. Many of our churches are experiencing 50 to 60 percent Sunday attendance compared to pre-pandemic numbers. When will they come back? Will they return? Who will return? We are uncertain.

How will the months or years of restrictions on our behavior—including how we experience church—impact us going forward? We are uncertain. How will all these changes impact diocesan structures throughout the Western world that were already feeling the strain of the cultural and social shifts over the last fifty years? We are uncertain.

These were my questions as I returned to parish ministry in August 2020 after a three-year stretch working half-time with Divine Renovation Ministry and half-time for my archdiocese. The conviction that the Covid-19 pandemic was not simply an interruption but a disruption was one factor that led me back to parish ministry. So much was uncertain. So much had changed, so much had to be learned, and so much had to be discovered.

The parish that I was asked to go to was one of many parishes in my diocese that had undergone a process of merging with other parishes. Like most of the parishes in my diocese, these five had been experiencing rapid decline for years and the demographic and financial outlook was not encouraging. On January 1, 2020, five communities of faith (four parishes and one mission to the Polish community) housed in four different locations became one new canonical and legal parish under the patronage of Our Lady of Guadalupe. Just over three months later, everything was shut down. I arrived on August 1 as pastor of a flock that was meager and masked, scattered and scared, confused and confounded, frustrated but faith-filled.

In the midst of uncertainty, we clung to the rock who is Christ and to that which remains unchanging in uncertain times. The invitation of Jesus to come and follow him, to be his disciples, echoes down through the ages to bring uncertainty to times of certainty and certainty to times of uncertainty. In the midst of so much change brought about by the pandemic and parish mergers, one thing I knew was certain was that the Lord was calling this new parish to become a community of missionary disciples.

This book was created from a number of homilies that I gave in my new parish in that first year. I am grateful to the editorial team at The Word Among Us for approaching me with the idea and doing an amazing job taking my reflections and transforming them into book form. The core message of these twelve chapters were initially preached to a community in the midst of the uncertainty of the pandemic, parish closures, and amalgamations. They were an attempt to cast a vision for a different way of being Church, to inspire and mobilize for our parish to embrace its missionary calling, and to help my parishioners through uncertainty.

I know that there are many parishes that are, or will be, going through similar experiences. I hope and pray that these reflections will assist you to respond personally and communally to the call of the Lord to be parishes that care for the flock, but, most of all, are ready to put out into the deep water to let down our nets for a catch. Parishes are people. Parishes are transformed when people are transformed, and all parishioners—by their yes to becoming missionary disciples in uncertain times—can impact a parish, even a dying parish, so that it will not simply survive but thrive!

1

When Overwhelming Need Meets Underwhelming Resources

Key Scripture: Matthew 14:13-21

B eginnings can be tenuous things.

I was recently appointed as pastor for Our Lady of Guadalupe Parish in Dartmouth, Nova Scotia. Previously I had spent many fruitful years as pastor of Saint Benedict Parish, launching and building Divine Renovation Ministry and later serving my brother priests in the Diocese of Halifax-Yarmouth. I began this new season of priestly ministry eager to apply the lessons I had learned over the past decade. My goal was to help Our Lady of Guadalupe Parish experience new life, new growth, and renewal. I also looked forward to learning new lessons alongside the amazing men and women of the parish.

The parish was a new community, composed of four previously separate parishes as well as a Polish mission. I decided to tour the four campuses when I first arrived. During that time, I met many different people and heard about the histories of each of the communities that now made up Our Lady of Guadalupe.

Normally when a priest comes to a parish as pastor, he has to absorb but one story and history; here I was trying to deal with five separate histories. I remember returning home that first night feeling overwhelmed—not only by the daunting task of transforming these separate parish cultures into one missionary focused community but also by the breadth of administrative demands. My tour that day revealed a total of fourteen buildings in various states of health across the four campuses. Fourteen!

I thought of the words of Jesus, "The harvest is abundant but the laborers are few" (Matthew 9:37). In our parish, the buildings were abundant, but the parishioners were few! I had excitedly launched into this new adventure only to come crashing into an inescapable reality: overwhelming need in a time of underwhelming resources. It presented a real challenge.

Somewhat nervously I prepared my first homily as pastor, and as I did, my apprehension started to melt away. The Gospel reading indicated by the lectionary was the story of the feeding of the five thousand from Matthew 14. You are probably familiar with that story.

Jesus, saddened by the death of John the Baptist, had withdrawn from the press of people and gone by boat to a deserted place. The crowds, however, followed him on foot. When Jesus stepped off the boat, he caught sight of the people, and his heart was moved with compassion. He spent time with them, healing their sick until late in the day. By then it was too late for them to go to the villages to buy food, so Jesus instructed his disciples to feed the crowd. When the twelve gathered up what they had, it amounted to only five loaves of bread and two fish.

Jesus told his disciples to bring the food to him. He said a blessing, broke the loaves, and gave the food to his disciples to distribute. Lo and behold, everyone ate their fill, and there were twelve baskets of food remaining.

This was a perfect reading for our parish's situation. Why? Because this Gospel passage speaks to the very human experience of being overwhelmed by need and realizing that we have an underwhelming amount of resources to deal with the need. As I reflected further, I realized that the powerful lessons in this Gospel apply not only to communities but also to our personal lives.

All of us, at one time or another, have experienced the unpleasant reality of being overwhelmed by something or someone. It might be a situation in the workplace or in the family, a broken or toxic relationship we cannot deal with, or some other challenge (or set of challenges) that life throws at us. If your heart is beating, you have faced the reality of having a need without having enough resources to meet that need.

Living Jesus' Response

In the feeding of the five thousand, Jesus models for us three responses we can offer when faced with an overwhelming need: (1) feel, (2) surrender, and (3) act.

Feel

Why am I starting with feelings? After all, the Church often says that we should not be ruled by our emotions, right?

Most of us, most of the time—even if we think of ourselves as incredibly rational people and deep thinkers—react not out of what we think but out of what we feel. Our emotions really do guide us. Have you ever reacted poorly to something that was objectively not that big a deal? And afterward tried to figure out why you responded with such anger, disappointment, or frustration? You probably acted out of your emotions. What we feel is important. In the feeding of the five thousand, Jesus acts from his feelings.

The story opens as Jesus retreats to a quiet, restful spot away from the press of people. He is probably exhausted, and he's grieving the beheading of his cousin John the Baptist, at the hands of King Herod. He has every right to be immersed in his own pain, his own questions, his own anxiety. To make matters worse, the secluded spot to which Jesus and his disciples retire is full of people. These are needy people, "intruding" on his space.

How does Jesus respond? What is his emotional reaction? He responds with compassion.

Now, I probably would not have reacted compassionately. I would have felt frustrated. I would have thrown a pity party, decorated with a bit of anger: "Poor me! I can't even get a simple day off!"

Yet Jesus lifts his eyes from his own pain, his own needs and concerns, and he truly sees the crowd in *their* need. Jesus confronts the reality of the crowd not with a litany of his own frustration. He goes beyond his own needs and preferences, and what he sees elicits his compassion.

The word St. Matthew uses to describe the compassion of Jesus is difficult to translate into English. When we think about feeling something intensely, we associate it with the heart. The word Matthew uses, however, comes from a Greek word, *splankna*, that originally referred to the intestinal region. Although being moved in the *splankna* can rightfully be translated as "from the heart," it has a more visceral meaning: something that is felt in the gut.

This is an important word for St. Luke. He uses it to describe how Jesus is moved when he encounters the widow of Nain at the funeral of her only son (Luke 7:13). It's the reaction of the good Samaritan as he beholds the broken man on the side of the road (Luke 10:33) and the father's reaction in the parable of the prodigal son (see Luke 15:20). *Splankna* is God's response to our need for salvation, proclaimed each morning in the Liturgy of the Hours when we sing about "the tender compassion of our God" (see Luke 1:78). This compassion may cause the heart to burn, but its origin is a few inches below the heart.

Compassion should be the first step for us—as parishes and as individuals. It is so easy, in these challenging and changing times, to be caught in the gravitational pull of our particular issues and agendas. We get locked in the prison of our uncertainty, pain, and anguish. But the Lord says to us, "Can you take your eyes off these things and just recognize the 'crowd' before you?"

Our parishes are often big, and even those on the smaller side have problems that seem quite large. These capture our attention. If we can take our eyes off ourselves, we can be free to truly see the suffering and reality of people around us. Only then can we become free to feel the compassion of God and share it with others.

Surrender

Jesus says one of the most ridiculous things in this Gospel story. The disciples are trying to be very practical. They come to Jesus and say, "Lord you know it's getting late. We should send the people away so they can get something to eat." Jesus responds: "You don't have to send them away; you give them something to eat!" The disciples are rightly a little put off.

After all, there were five thousand men to feed, plus the women and children. All the disciples had were five measly loaves of bread and two skinny fish! Jesus' command must have sounded completely absurd. The disciples knew that these provisions could never meet the overwhelming need of the crowd. What Jesus asked of them was not humanly possible.

The same is true of our communities and of our own lives. What Jesus asks of us as parishes—that we become fruitful in mission—is humanly impossible. The same is true of what he asks of us personally: that we become like him!

We do not have enough resources to accomplish these things. We could be the richest, most well-endowed parish in the world, and we still could not do it. We could have all the wealth and power in the world, and we still would not accomplish what the Lord wants us to do. And the truth is, most of our communities are not rich, and most of us do not possess a great deal of power. We will always have inadequate resources relative to God's plan for us.

However, Jesus instructs his disciples in the Gospel story to do something specific: to bring him their inadequate store of food. Out of those five loaves and two fish, Jesus provides abundantly. For our part, as long as we consider the resources we have—our "loaves" and our "fish"—too meager to make a difference, we will fail to appreciate that the Lord can multiply them. When we hold back what little we have from the one who wants to give us everything good, he cannot work through us as he desires.

But if we surrender to Jesus what we have—our hopes, our dreams, our sense of nostalgia, our limited strength—Jesus multiplies and magnifies our simple offering, making the impossible possible. Through us Jesus feeds the multitude. He has done it before, and he will do it again.

We need to definitively declare that our parishes and our whole lives belong to Jesus. It is only through this kind of surrender that we truly experience the abundance of God's kingdom.

Act

We act not simply for action's sake. We need to act *in obedience* to the Lord.

"

If we surrender to Jesus what
we have—our hopes, our dreams,
our sense of nostalgia, our limited
strength—Jesus multiplies and
magnifies our simple offering,
making the impossible possible.

Think about this miracle. Jesus did not make the Sign of the Cross over the fish and, all of a sudden, BANG, a mountain of fish appeared. He did not make the Sign of the Cross over the bread and then BANG, an enormous basket of bread fell out of the sky. Out of such an abundance of food, the disciples would have freely fed everyone. That would have been easy. It would be easy to see the miracle first and then act.

Instead Jesus sent the disciples into the crowd with basically empty baskets. They were probably thinking that they were "dead meat"—or at least that they would look like complete idiots as they walked out with virtually nothing in their baskets. And yet as they went out in obedience, God performed a miracle: he fed the multitude.

The lesson is clear for us, as individuals and as parishes: We cannot wait for some perfect future or some perfect set of resources. We must act in obedience, believing that the Lord is going to come behind us and provide what we need.

Beginning the Journey

For now I would like to focus on the first principle Jesus shows us: to feel. We explored the fact that Jesus had an emotional reaction when he saw the crowd. That is what I would like you to have: an emotional reaction. If we want to create thriving, vibrant parish communities, we must stop focusing only on our concerns and truly confront the reality of our brothers and sisters who live alongside us—not simply those whom we worship with but our neighbors, friends, and coworkers. I want to invite you to get out of the four walls of your church to walk the streets within the geographical boundaries of your parish.

Walk with your spouse or another family member, with a friend, or with one of your neighbors. You can spend time in areas with which you are familiar or get in your car or on a bus and range further afield, to places within your parish boundaries where you have not spent much time. I want you to see the joys, griefs, and struggles that make up the lives of your brothers and sisters. And I want you to have an emotional reaction.

This is the "homework" I gave the people of my own parish. I did it as well. I walked over six miles and tried to open myself to what was around me. As I walked, I prayed: "Lord, help me see what you see. Help me feel your compassion for 'the crowd.'"

Friends, let us be moved in the deepest parts of our person, in our *splankna*. Like Jesus, let us be moved in our gut! If we do not care about the crowds "out there," then what is the point of gathering "here," in our church buildings? How will what happens inside impact the world outside?

I am reminded of something Pope Francis said:

If something should rightly disturb us and trouble our consciences, it is the fact that so many of our brothers and sisters are living without the strength, light and consolation born of friendship with Jesus Christ, without a community of faith to support them, without meaning and a goal in life. More than by fear of going astray, my hope is that we will be moved by the fear of remaining shut up within structures which give us a false sense of security, within rules which make us harsh judges, within habits which make us feel safe, while at our door people are starving and Jesus does not tire of saying to us: "Give them something to eat" (Mark 6:37).[1]

Questions for Reflection and Discussion

Take some time to reflect on the following questions, whether you are reading this book privately or reading it as part of a group. If you are making this journey with a group, share your answers with one another.

1. As you prayerfully read through the key Scripture passage for this chapter, what words, phrases, or images caught your attention or drew your focus? What might the Lord be communicating to you through them?

2. If you journeyed around your local neighborhood, what "moved your gut"? What situations did you witness that made you rejoice? What moved you with compassion as you paid special attention to the wants and needs of others?

3. Based on those experiences, what can you do as an individual to meet the needs of the people you encountered? What godly response to their situations can you offer? Take a moment and reflect on how your parish, as a faith community, might respond to specific needs in an individual and systemic way.

2

The Power of God

Fifteen years ago, I bought my first-ever television.
Previous to that, I had always lived in a rectory where
there was a common room. For the first time, I actually had
a living space with my own sitting room—but no TV! So I
saved my money, and then one night I went to the store. I
was filled with excitement as I thought about what I wanted:
a fifty-inch plasma television. You do not see those things
around much anymore. They were the first generation of
flat-screen TVs, and they weighed a ton.

In fact, the fifty-inch TV I purchased weighed a monstrous
hundred pounds. I was not deterred, even when I discovered that the box would not fit in my car. After some quick
thinking and with the help of the salesman, I took the TV
out of its box and placed it directly in my car.

Driving home, I could barely contain my excitement as
I thought about setting it up. I planned to enlist the aid of
one of the other priests to help me carry the TV into the
kitchen, around the corner, and up two flights of stairs to

my room. When I made it back to the rectory, however, no one else was home. I *really* wanted to set up my TV that night, so I thought I'd give it a try by myself.

Somehow I managed to lift this hundred-pound piece of fragile equipment out of my car and maneuver it up the stairs to the back door of the rectory. Even more impressively, I balanced the weight of this monstrosity on my knee while I fished in my pocket for the key that would open the screen door. I made it into the kitchen, set the television down on the table, and rested a bit.

A few deep breaths later, I went for it. I lifted that TV around the corner and managed to go up one flight of steps—and then another flight. Here I was, actually doing it, despite the awkward bulk and weight of this television. But as I turned another corner to enter into my sitting room, I realized all of a sudden that I was not going to make it.

I still remember that feeling: it was as if I simply ran out of strength. I could not carry the load anymore, and I realized that I was going to drop the TV. Thanks be to God, in that moment I saw beside me my couch, right by the door. With my last bit of strength, I turned and dropped the TV right onto that couch.

The safety of this old television is not the point of the story. The point of this story is coming to terms with the experience of "I cannot do it" and the reality of "I am not strong enough." We can experience this type of weakness not only in the physical dimensions of our lives but in the emotional, psychological, and spiritual dimensions as well. We have all, at some point in our lives, come to that moment when life and its challenges became overwhelming, when we simply felt exhausted, when we ran out of resources. Perhaps the thought hit us like a slap in the face: "I can't do this anymore. I can't stay the course or go the distance.

"I am going to drop the TV."

St. Paul experienced this. We can see that from his Letter to the Philippians. Paul wrote this epistle when he was in prison, literally in chains.

Being in a Roman prison cell at that time was deeply unpleasant, to put it mildly. And you had to rely on your friends for food and clothing. Paul's friends in the city of Philippi sent one of their "parishioners," Epaphroditus, to the prison to take care of Paul's needs. Disaster soon struck, however: Epaphroditus fell ill and nearly died.

You can almost feel St. Paul's struggles: no food, no clothing, chained up in a Roman prison, with his friend close to dying. In this letter, Paul writes from experience that he knows what it means to have plenty and to go without. He knew true deprivation.

Clearly, Paul was familiar with the experience of not having enough strength. But he didn't let that reality define his situation. In chapter four of this letter, he writes something profound, strong, and challenging: "I have the strength for everything through him who empowers me" (Philippians 4:13).

I believe this! I believe that experiencing our weakness—coming to grips with the cold, hard truth that we are not strong enough—is essential if we are to experience the power of God in our life. We only unlock the strength of God when we know, in the depths of our being, that we cannot carry everything on our own shoulders.

St. Paul wrote his amazing words during a time of great trial and difficulty. In fact, in this powerful epistle, he managed to talk about joy sixteen times.

Unpacking the Truth

Let us break down that Scripture passage a bit further. A common translation of this passage is "I can do all things through him who strengthens me" (NRSVCE). Translated more literally, it means something like this: "I am strong in all things in him who empowers me" (my translation). Although these translations are similar, they have a bit of a difference. The first begins, "I can do all things," while my translation says, "I am strong in all things." The first stresses the *doing*, and the second stresses the *being*.

We tend to do much better focusing on the *being* side of existence rather than on the *doing*. Furthermore, focusing on doing is kind of misleading. Even with God right by our side, there are lots of things that we will never be able to accomplish. In fact, we may experience failure even when doing the Lord's work. When the Lord is with us, however, we can be strong and endure those difficult times.

Another critical difference between the translations is in the use of prepositional phrases. The first translation highlights that we can be strong *through* him, while the second translation (mine) states that we can be strong *in* him. The truth is that not all prepositions are created equal!

I really appreciate the use of the word "in." I can do things *through* God, but that almost reduces God to a utility, as if God is useful to us in the way that a car or electricity is useful and practical. And that connotes a kind of distance between us and the God who cherishes us.

Being strong *in* him, however, reveals intimacy. St. Paul often describes the Christian life as being life in Christ (see Colossians 1:27, for example). Christ is in us, and we are in him. Jesus himself, in John's Gospel, says:

> Remain in me, as I remain in you. Just as a branch cannot bear fruit on its own unless it remains on the vine, so neither can you unless you remain in me. I am the vine, you are the branches. Whoever remains in me and I in him will bear much fruit, because without me you can do nothing. (John 15:4-5)

The Lord does want us to do things through him, but even more he wants us to live *in* him. He wants to make his home within us.

Finally, there is a difference between the phrase "strengthens me" versus "empowers me." On the surface, this might not be apparent, but there are definite nuances. If we say that God strengthens us, it is almost as if we accomplish something with God that we could have done all by ourselves without him—only not as well. Whereas when God empowers us, he is the source of our ability to accomplish the work. In fact, the very literal translation of this passage from Philippians speaks of "he who continuously puts his power within me." When

God empowers us, we can do things that we could never have done before.

Think of smart phones. These are amazing inventions that can do complicated tasks. There is one thing they cannot do, however, and that is to charge themselves. They simply do not have that ability. Their power must come from somewhere else; they must be empowered. And depending upon how old your phone is, it might have to be continuously empowered! If it has a charge though, the sky is practically the limit in terms of what it can accomplish—things it could never do without that power.

The same is true in the Christian life. God empowers us continuously, so that we are able to be strong no matter the circumstances, challenges, difficulties, pain, suffering, and disappointments of life. You can be strong in him: in Jesus, who constantly puts his power in you. Jesus told his disciples after his resurrection, "I am sending the promise of my Father upon you; but stay in the city until you are clothed with power from on high" (Luke 24:49).

The key here is to examine ourselves with brutal honesty and ask some difficult questions: "What truly is beyond my strength?" and "Where do I exhibit weakness?"

The beautiful reality is that the Lord can illuminate our minds if we ask him to reveal answers to these questions—not so that we can throw a pity party for ourselves but so that we can lift up our weaknesses to him in prayer. When we profess our weaknesses to God and ask for his strength, we know that he listens and responds. Trusting in the Lord,

"

You can be strong in him: in Jesus,

who constantly puts his power in you.

we then can take the next steps on the sometimes long road of transformation.

As we face struggles in our personal lives and difficult times as parish communities, let us recognize that our experiences of being overwhelmed, of recognizing that we do not have enough strength, are actually good things. When we truly know that we do not have the strength to carry on, that is when we can turn to the Lord, open our hearts to him, and truly have the experience of being strong in him who constantly puts his power in us.

Questions for Reflection and Discussion

1. Prayerfully read the key Scripture passage for this chapter. What words, phrases, or images caught your attention? What might the Lord be communicating to you through these?

2. Have you experienced a time in your life when your own strength, talents, and gifts weren't enough to see you through a challenge or difficulty and you needed to rely on God's strength? What happened?

3. Take a moment to reflect on the life of your parish community. Has your parish experienced a challenge or difficulty that required the strength of God? How did the parish seek this strength, and what were the results?

4. This chapter talks about doing things in God's strength, coming from an intimacy with the Lord. Have you had intimate moments with the Lord? How would you describe them to others?

3

Comforting the Afflicted and Afflicting the Comfortable

Key Scripture: Matthew 14:22-33

Someone once said that the job of the preacher is to comfort the afflicted and afflict the comfortable. While I completely agree with this insight, it is one thing to believe it and another to actually do it.

One of the challenges of a preacher is knowing who is who: who needs to be comforted, and who needs to be afflicted? In reality, the challenge goes much deeper. It is not so much "who is who" but rather "when is when." The truth is that we all, at different times in our lives, need to be comforted, and at other times, we need to be afflicted or challenged.

Think about it. If we are only consoled or comforted, we can become soft, incapable of dealing with the harsh realities of this life. Likewise, if we are only challenged or afflicted, we can become hard, embittered, and even broken. To really mature and become the people we are called to be—to live life to the full—we need some of both, comfort and affliction.

Jesus demonstrated this reality in the famous Gospel story in which Peter walked on water. After Jesus finished praying, the story tells us, he went down to the lake. The disciples were in a boat several miles from shore, and the wind was against them. Waves battered the boat.

That image is quite a metaphor for life. Who hasn't felt powerless, as if wind and waves were battering them, far from any help as they tried to make it through life? Who hasn't felt as if they were trying to make headway against winds so powerful that, no matter how hard they tried, they could not make any progress?

A number of years ago, while visiting friends in Cape Breton Island, I decided to go kayaking on Bras d'Or Lake. My initial crossing was an easy journey, to my surprise. Then I tried to turn around. That's when I discovered that my first trip across the lake was easy because the wind was at my back. Now the wind was against me, and I had to fight it. In addition, the current was stronger, and the waves were much bigger. No matter how hard I paddled, I did not make much progress. In fact, I was driven off course.

Then I realized something that I would have known if I had checked the map beforehand: the Bras d'Or Lake is not a lake at all but an estuary open to the ocean. Essentially it's an arm of the Atlantic Ocean! If I didn't keep up the fight against the wind and the waves, I could end up in open water and on my way to Newfoundland. It was a scary and exhausting experience.

Though it took me a long time, I eventually arrived safely back where I had started. And I have never forgotten that experience of being battered by waves, with the wind against me, far from land.

Kayaking in the Barque of Peter

In a similar fashion, as the Church we might feel that we are facing into the wind and losing ground. The Church has been through a lot in these past thirty or so years: battered by crises and scandals. We might feel far from land. Much of what was familiar to us has been torn away, especially during the pandemic. Church life can be disorienting—particularly in dioceses going through amalgamation and retrenching, whereby parish names and even parish identities change so as to combine limited resources.

The system we have inherited as a Church is built on the presumption that the wind would be at our back. Yet the wind often seems to be against us. Here I refer to the wind of culture. Forty or fifty years ago, you could presume that most people thought believing in God and going to church were pretty good things. You could also presume that most people in North America had a Christian worldview. Today, however, you cannot presume those things; you can presume the opposite. The wind is against us.

Regardless of whether we experience the storms of life as individuals or as parish communities, one thing remains absolutely true: Jesus comes toward us, as he came toward the disciples being battered in their tiny boat. He speaks the same words to us that he spoke two thousand years ago: "Take courage, it is I; do not be afraid" (Matthew 14:27).

Notice that Jesus did not immediately calm the storm. First he revealed his presence to the disciples in the midst of the storm. He does the same for us. Today he is revealing his presence to us, individually and as parish communities, in the midst of life's storms. Jesus wants to comfort us in our afflictions.

If we continue reading that Gospel story, however, we see that Jesus also afflicts the comfortable—in this case, Peter. You might think that Peter was not all that comfortable in the storm-tossed boat. But when the Lord assured the disciples that they need not be afraid. Peter took advantage of the moment. "Lord" Peter said, "if it is you, command me to come to you on the water" (Matthew 14:28).

Jesus replied, "Come. Leave the safety of the boat. Come and walk on water." Peter got out of the boat to walk on the stormy sea, but he began to sink when he saw how strong the wind was. Jesus immediately stretched out his hand to help him.

Together these situations—the disciples afflicted in the boat and Peter stepping out of the boat—offer a powerful metaphor for the life to which Christ calls us. We need not be paralyzed by our fears and afflictions in the midst of the storms of life, nor complacent about what is comfortable or seems safe. When we cling to Jesus himself, nothing can paralyze us.

We must ask ourselves, as we hear the consolation of the Lord, are we also open to the affliction of the Lord? Can

"

Can we hear Jesus calling us to get out of the boat, to let go of the familiar? We need to hear his voice saying, "Take heart! It is I; do not be afraid."

we listen for the voice of the Lord, even as he invites us to change in the midst of life's storms that we're experiencing right now? Can we hear Jesus calling us to get out of the boat, to let go of the familiar? We need to hear his voice saying, "Take heart! It is I; do not be afraid." We need to hear his invitation to get out of the boat.

We will only encounter the comfort of the Lord and accept affliction if we are rooted in the experience of prayer. This prayer is not so much about our talking to God—telling him what we want him to do—but rather a matter of listening to the Lord. Scripture offers a privileged place to listen to the Lord, so I want to give you a bit of homework for this week: Go to the key Scripture passage of this chapter (Matthew 14:22-33), and spend ten minutes praying through it.

First quiet yourself, and ask the Lord to open your mind and your heart. Then read the passage in a reflective, gentle way, allowing Jesus to speak to you as an individual and as a member of a parish going through life's storms. When we open ourselves to Jesus' words of comfort and affliction on a regular basis, we become the people God calls us to be and the parish community that God empowers us to be.

Questions for Reflection and Discussion

1. As you prayerfully read through the Scripture passage for this chapter, what words, phrases, or images caught your attention or drew your focus?

2. What is Jesus saying to you about the personal storms you face? What emotions did you experience as you prayed with the passage? What images came to mind? Write these down, so you can reflect on them later.

3. Make a list of the challenges your parish faces, and see yourself surrendering them to the Lord. Receive his consolation. Then ask him what he wants you to do about these challenges.

4

The Monkey Trap,
Repentance, and the Cross

Key Scriptures: Matthew 16:21-27; Romans 12:1-2

Did you ever think you could learn something from a monkey?

In many countries of the world, people catch monkeys using a simple technique. They take a coconut, drill a hole in it, put a tasty morsel of food inside, and fasten it to a tree. When the monkey comes along, it reaches inside the coconut to grab the food. The hole is big enough to allow the monkey to place its hand inside, but when the monkey makes a fist to snatch the treat, it cannot pull its hand out. Unwilling to drop its prize, the monkey stays there, trying to pull out its fist, while its captors arrive.

Here's the crazy thing: the monkey is not trapped by a barrier but by an idea. If it would just let go of the food, it could be free. Monkeys, however, have learned that holding on to food is a good thing to do. And it is, until it's not.

In Matthew's Gospel, Jesus says something extraordinary: "Whoever wishes to come after me must deny himself, take up his cross, and follow me. For whoever wishes to save his life will lose it, but whoever loses his life for my sake will find it" (Matthew 16:24-25). Like those monkeys clinging to their food, if we cling to a false understanding of life— if we fail to deny ourselves and take up our cross—we will lose whatever life we have.

This idea of taking up your cross is very familiar to Christians. The image of the cross is familiar as well. We wear it around our necks as a symbol of hope, and life, and love. Remember, however, that Jesus spoke these words before his crucifixion and resurrection.

For Jesus' contemporaries, the cross was an instrument of torturous execution and a symbol of Roman power, oppression, and authority. The cross struck fear and dread into people. It would be a very odd thing to wear around one's neck. Imagine if you saw someone today walking around with a hangman's noose around their neck!

We sometimes forget the actual impact of the image of the cross. Even the idea of taking up your cross has lost some of its original power. In our contemporary Christian spirituality, we have often interpreted that expression to mean that we should put up with the hardships of life, the difficulties and unavoidable suffering. We "offer it up" and take up our cross. Yet Jesus proposes something more radical with his words. In fact, his listeners would have heard his invitation this way: "Come and die. If you wish to be my disciple, come and die." Jesus calls his followers to embrace a dying process.

Jesus spoke of this often in his teaching, using various images to drive home his point. He talked about the seed that needed to fall into the ground and die; otherwise it would not bear fruit (see John 12:24). He spoke about his own life and ministry in this way as well (John 14:27-31). If we reflect on our lives in general, on our own personal growth and our relationships, we see that there is truth here. We know that a key part of maturing is to die to our need for immediate gratification and a primary focus on ourselves. That is the difference between an adult and a child.

We also know that for a relationship to flourish and grow, we have to die to that selfishness within us that makes it "all about me." Think of any successful and fruitful marriage. In order to bear fruit, the spouses have to come together and die to themselves. If they do not, then the marriage itself dies.

The same thing applies to the spiritual life, as we seek to die to that reality called sin and to the things that lead us away from God. This is true of us personally, and it is also true of us corporately, as a Church. If we don't actively embrace the death that leads to life, then the life that leads to death will embrace us.

What might that mean for our parishes? I do not know. This will be a process of discovery that pastors and their teams must explore together with their communities. I don't know details, and I don't know with certainty all the various implications, but I *do* know that we must move beyond the status quo. We cannot simply continue living as parishes the way we have historically. Our current context demands a fresh response.

We have to embrace change, and change is always painful. Here it is an embrace of the paschal mystery, a taking up of our communal crosses so that we might die to that which is no longer fruitful and begin to bear fruit in new ways. If we want to bear the fruit of change, however, we cannot avoid the pain of change.

Transformation

I spoke similar words to my own parish as we began this journey of change together. I had the grace of coming into the newly combined communities that made up Our Lady of Guadalupe parish right at the beginning, and so I saw the parish as one. Nevertheless I went out to the locations that previously made up the separate parishes and mission, in order to get to know those parishioners—their hopes, their dreams for the future, and the history of their communities. As I did so, I discovered something very interesting.

Three of the four previous parishes were small; together they made up only a third of the new parish. However, the people in those smaller communities were very familiar with this experience of dying and of making sacrifices—in some ways more than the people of the fourth and largest community.

For example, a number of years before, one of the smaller parishes lost a resident priest. More recently, they saw the closure of their parish office. And as the pandemic continued, they no longer had a Sunday Mass in their parish church. These folks have lived under the

"

We have to embrace the paschal
mystery, a taking up of our communal
crosses so that we might die to that
which is no longer fruitful and begin
to bear fruit in new ways.

shadow of their buildings being closed down and their community dying.

The people of the larger and more resourced community, on the other hand, have experienced little of this over the years. They still have their parish office and their priests; even the Mass times have remained the same. Because of this reality, the larger group of the new parish, which made up 60 percent of parishioners in the newly combined parish, had unintentionally communicated to the smaller groups that the real answer to making change was to close down and be absorbed into us.

St. Peter's Church, which housed this largest parish, is now the main church for the combined parish. It is the biggest church of the four: during Covid and the necessary social distancing, it could seat 120 to 150 people, and the other churches could only seat between 40 and 70. When Sunday Mass resumed, we had Mass only at the St. Peter's location because of its size.

Behind the presider's chair at this church was a huge yellow, orange, and green tapestry featuring stick people on a boat with their arms raised. The boat represented the Barque of Peter. Some people loved it, some used to love it, and others thought it was pretty ugly.

One day during prayer, I was thinking about ways we could unify the parish. The tapestry, like the church building itself, was unique in our diocese. It represented the last fifty years of parish history and identity, as the church had been rebuilt after a fire destroyed the original building in 1966. Yet we were a new parish. None of the constitutive parishes existed any longer.

I thought of the time I visited the Shrine of Our Lady of Guadalupe in Mexico City and saw the tilma on the wall behind the altar. That's when the idea came to me: we should frame a high-quality image of Our Lady of Guadalupe and hang it above the presider's chair. In order to do this, however, we would have to cover the tapestry.

We went to work and consulted with a professional interior designer. Several months later it was complete. Beautiful cream curtains covered the tapestry, and in the center hung the image of Our Lady, the patroness of our new parish, illumined by careful lighting.

The reaction was swift. The vast majority of parishioners thought the new image was breathtakingly beautiful. The tableau also made the new identity of our combined parish real for many. For those who came from the three smaller locations and those who were new to the parish, this change helped them feel at home, not like visitors in someone else's spiritual home.

Some of the pillars of the St. Peter's community still held a nostalgic connection to the old tapestry. However, while they admitted that they would miss it, several told me that it had not struck them before this time that St. Peter's Parish no longer existed. The invitation to transformation was not just for those "other parishes" but for the entire community. Having members of the combined parishes worshipping at St. Peter's post-Covid helped cement this transformation. The Eucharist strengthens our unity.

The Place of Sacrifice

The dynamic of absorption is often present when a diocese tries to combine larger and smaller communities. To a certain degree, the temptation that every community must face when asked to die to its old identity and embrace a new one is to think that the "other" parish community should be absorbed into "us." I don't think this is the way God wants us to go about this process of dying and rising. But how do we know the path the Lord wants us to take on this journey?

The Letter to the Romans 12:1-2—this chapter's second key Scripture—provides an answer. St. Paul writes that we can know the will of God through offering ourselves as "living sacrifice[s]." This becomes our "spiritual worship," which God finds pleasing. When we offer our whole selves as a sacrifice, we will stop being conformed to worldly ways of thinking, and we will be transformed by the grace of God, as he renews our minds. It is only in this renewal of our minds that we can come to know the will of God.

To offer ourselves as living sacrifices means nothing less than to accept the invitation of Jesus to come and die. At every Mass, we gather around the altar. Consider that in ancient times, the Jews offered animal sacrifices on an altar; they reserved the altar for this ritual. In fact, the Hebrew word for "altar" means "place for slaughter or sacrifice."

And so Jesus asks us to put everything on the altar, to lay everything down for him in a death to self. This invitation to authentic worship—to offer ourselves as living sacrifices, to come and die—is extended not only to small parish communities but equally to larger ones. Only when we, as whole communities, accept this invitation will we truly be able to discern the will of God for the future of our parishes.

Questions for Reflection and Discussion

1. Prayerfully read through the key Scripture passages for this chapter. What words, phrases, or images drew your focus? What do you think the Lord is trying to communicate to you through them?

2. What is your general reaction to change? Do you tend to avoid change, preferring to rely on things that have historically worked? Or do you like to try new ways of doing things, new approaches? Why do you prefer one way rather than the other?

3. Recalling the story of the monkey trap, what things in your life do you hold tightly in your grasp? What might the Lord be asking you to surrender to him so that you might live in greater freedom?

4. What aspects of your parish life do you hold tightly and not want to see change? In other words, what ideas keep you trapped? What might the Lord be asking you to surrender to him about these areas, so that your parish can grow into a more fruitful, evangelizing parish?

5

The Power of Mercy

Key Scripture: Matthew 18:21-36

Twelve years ago, I was sitting by the Sea of Galilee in Israel. It was my first trip to the Holy Land. Toward the end of my ten days there, I had received a text on my phone. I discovered, to my horror, that my cell phone company was billing me $780 for data roaming.

I didn't really know what data roaming was at the time. All I understood was that I could use my cell phone overseas to get e-mails and do a whole bunch of fun things. I did not have any idea what this might actually cost. To make matters worse, I had been playing a humorous video on my phone repeatedly the day before. For some reason, I thought that smartphones worked like computers: once you download a video, it remains on your device, and you can access it without downloading it again. I didn't realize that every time I pressed play on my phone, I was downloading the data again and racking up another forty-to-fifty-dollar bill.

This discovery, quite naturally, made me sick to my stomach.

A few days later, I returned to Canada and called my cell phone provider. I pleaded stupidity and asked them to erase the download charges on my bill. They said they would consider my case and get back to me. Two days later, they called to say that they felt sorry for me and were going to forgive the entire $780 debt. I was elated! It felt amazing to have my debt forgiven.

I share this story because it reminds me of Jesus' parable of the unforgiving servant. A servant who owes his master a great deal of money (ten thousand talents) begs forgiveness of his debt, and the master agrees. That servant then encounters a fellow servant who owes him a mere hundred denarii. The first servant grabs his fellow servant by the throat. The harried servant begs his attacker for mercy and patience, and he assures him that he will repay the debt in full eventually. But the servant whose master forgave his debt refuses to show mercy to his fellow servant. He received mercy from his master but refuses to show mercy. The master finds out about this, has his guards seize the unforgiving servant, and hands him over to the torturers.

The obvious point of the parable is that if we come to God asking for mercy and forgiveness, we should offer mercy and forgiveness to others. We should forgive one another because God has forgiven us. This is a powerful lesson, but there is much more to this parable than we might see at first glance, because most of us are not experts in ancient Near Eastern systems of currency. The real impact of this Gospel reading lies in the relative amount of money in play.

The first debtor owes his master ten thousand talents. One talent was worth more than fifteen years' salary of an average wage earner, so that first servant owed his master at least 150,000 years' worth of salary. In today's currency, the servant could owe his master six billion US dollars. That is an incredible amount of money.

Yet the first man begs his master to be patient, and he will pay him back. How? That servant probably works at the equivalent of McDonald's. His debt is an impossible debt to pay back.

And that is the whole point.

God is infinitely good and gracious. Sin is an offense against God, and because of God's infinite nature, it is in a real sense an infinite offense that creates an infinite debt. Therefore when God forgives us, he erases an infinite debt. Scripture tells us that God paid that debt not through any sum of silver or gold but through the precious blood of Jesus (see 1 Peter 1:18-19). This is the mercy we have received from the Father in Jesus Christ.

The second servant owed the first servant a hundred denarii. A single denarius was worth one day's wage. So this servant owed a hundred days' wages, perhaps thirteen thousand US dollars today. That is not a small amount by any stretch of the imagination, but it pales in comparison to six billion.

Think about the magnitude of what God has forgiven us. Now think about how often we keep accounts of others. Maybe we keep score regarding their failings or make entries in a ledger detailing all the ways they owe us. We hold on to petty resentments and bitterness and unforgiveness.

Whom do we most resemble? Probably that first servant.

In one sense, this parable sheds light on the fact that holding on to that junk really is ridiculous, because we have been forgiven so much. If we are not overwhelmed by what we have received, we will be overwhelmed by a sense of what we have lost. It is so easy for that dynamic to creep into our relationships.

Whenever I hear this parable, I recall that moment of debt forgiveness in my life. I felt pretty elated for a few days. I was probably more generous and patient and kind than usual. But eventually I stopped remembering what I had been given and forgiven. I went back to my normal way of being, focusing too often on what others owed me.

This dynamic can come into all our relationships: with our families and spouses, in our workplaces, in our parish activities. We slowly stop being generous and gracious because we forget what we have received and notice only what we have lost.

In this life, the experience of loss is incredibly real. Yet we have a choice, don't we? We can either focus on what we have lost or focus on what we have received. Where we focus can impact us as members of the Church.

This has been especially true in recent years. Think about the huge problems we have now as a Church because of the changes in contemporary culture over the last several decades. Our infrastructure, our buildings, our ways of doing things have ceased to work, and it's really taking a toll on us. We experience it in the declining numbers in our parishes, the aging of our congregations, the decay of our buildings—all results of the shifts in society. We are experiencing loss after loss.

The closing and combining of our parishes also bring with them a sense of loss of identity. Maybe we are a part of a new parish, or we have become a blended community with a new name, and we mourn the loss of our particular community. Or perhaps we struggle with our losses around the Covid-19 pandemic. Most of us lost access to the Eucharist and the other sacraments for many months, and then, when we could gather together in one building, we had to wear masks, keep distant from one another, not touch each other, not even sing.

Yet in spite of all that loss, nothing compares to what we have received and continue to receive. We have the Lord himself. We have his forgiveness. We have the assurance of eternal life.

The questions for us, in our experience of Church, are the same as in our everyday lives: Are we going to focus on our losses? Are we going to be bitter and angry people, grabbing others by the throat and shouting at them to "pay what you owe"? Or will we choose to be overwhelmed by what God has given us?

Take some time this week—maybe ten minutes a day will do—to prayerfully read through our key Scripture passage. Ask the Lord to help you recognize and be overwhelmed by his grace and mercy to you. He has forgiven your infinite debt simply because you have asked for his mercy and forgiveness.

Open yourself up to the magnitude of what you have been given and forgiven. Then ask the Lord to give you insight

"

Open yourself up to the
magnitude of what you have
been given and forgiven.

into areas of your life where you are still counting the cost, into relationships where you may hold others by the throat and need to forgive, and into losses that you have not been able to surrender to God.

In the end, ask the Lord to set you free from any sense of loss, as an individual and as a member of the Church, so that you might experience the Lord's transformation. Then you can become a person who is powerfully overwhelmed by all you have received through the mercy of God.

Questions for Reflection and Discussion

1. While reading through the key Scripture passage for this chapter, what words, phrases, or images caught your attention or drew your focus? What might the Lord be communicating to you through them?

2. Have you ever had an experience of someone showing you mercy and forgiveness when you truly did not deserve it? What was that experience like? Did it have a long-term effect on you?

3. Make a list of all the things you have received from the Lord, including major experiences of his forgiveness. Then bring these to prayer throughout the week, and specifically thank God for each one of them. As you finish your week of gratitude, notice what effect, if any, that prayerful attention to thanking the Lord has had on you. Has it changed anything about your life or your prayer? If so, what?

4. Spend some time this week making a list of ways that the Lord has blessed your parish. Be as specific as possible. Then bring that list to prayer, and thank the Lord for what he has done for your parish.

5. Is God asking you to show mercy and forgiveness to specific people or in specific situations? What can you do this week to start that process of forgiveness?

6

Who Says
God Is Fair?

Key Scriptures: Isaiah 55:6-9; Matthew 20:1-16

I'm not the most patient person in the world. Waiting in line is one of the experiences I like the least.

Last year I was flying into another country on a fairly small plane. I was the first person off the plane when we landed, and I made a beeline for the customs hall. I made some quick assessments as to which lines were the shortest and were moving the fastest and joined what looked to be the most efficient line. Great—except that once I joined that line, it stopped moving.

I swiftly recalculated and moved to another line. No sooner had I joined that one then it too stopped. Frustrated yet still hopeful, I saw another line that was processing people and got to the back of that line. As I started to advance, I felt a bit of relief. Then that line too stopped moving.

At this point, I was too embarrassed to move again. I stuck it out in that very slow line. In the end, although I was first off the plane, I was the last to leave customs.

Indeed, "the last will be first, and the first will be last" (Matthew 20:16). That is what Jesus tells us in the parable of a landowner who goes out into the marketplace to hire workers. First he goes at six o'clock in the morning and hires some laborers. Then he comes back to hire more—at nine o'clock, noon, three o'clock, and finally five o'clock.

In Jesus' time, the workday went from about six in the morning to six in the evening. Thus the workers hired at five only had to labor one hour before they received their pay. The landowner instructs his manager to pay these workers first and to pay them as much as the workers he hired early in the morning, who broke their backs laboring all day in the heat. Does that seem fair? Should those who show up for an hour of work receive the same pay as those who diligently labor all day?

If we are honest with ourselves, we would say, "No way!" That situation offends our human sense of justice. It does not make any sense.

Yet in our first key Scripture, from Isaiah, the Lord is clear:

For my thoughts are not your thoughts,
    nor are your ways my ways. . . .
For as the heavens are higher than the earth,
    so are my ways higher than your ways
    my thoughts higher than your thoughts. (Isaiah 55:8-9)

Although the instinct for justice, especially distributive justice or fairness, is a God-given instinct, mere human justice does not always dovetail with divine justice. Frankly, in the kingdom of God, people get what they do not deserve and often *don't get what they do deserve*. God's mercy turns our human understanding of fairness on its head. We are in the world but called to not be of the world, and so we must wrestle with the reality of a divine justice that does not always seem fair.

Many of us are like the workers who have come late to the field. We have received not what we deserve but what the Lord in his infinite generosity desires for us. We have received redemption and the possibility of peace, justice, and eternal union with God (things that are not ours by right). Coming to terms with this means embracing authentic humility, which recognizes that everything good we have received comes from God and is a true gift. Living from that perspective, it becomes easier to surrender our personal wishes, preferences, and desires and to avoid any sense of ownership of our gifts, goods, and treasure.

The Parish Vineyard

I want to bring that concept into our understanding of parish life. In most human organizations and enterprises, those who were first on the ground, those who have been working the longest at the company, tend to be the most important people in that structure. It makes a lot of sense; in fact, it seems right and fair that the people who have invested the most in something have a controlling voice and more authority over that enterprise. I don't think too many of us would disagree with that statement. But when it comes to life in the Church, we are not working only from a human sense of justice—especially in light of Jesus' parable.

Sometimes in a parish, parishioners who have been there the longest can "own" the identity and mission of "their" parish in a way that becomes exclusive. They can begin to see new parishioners as threats. These new parishioners can easily become "those people over there," and any attempt by "those people" to get involved or be a part of the work of the parish is met with resistance.

This is a great challenge for us, because the Church is a living organism. If it doesn't receive new people, if it doesn't have new blood, it will cease to be healthy. When a parish becomes unhealthy, it will not grow or bear fruit. Therefore we must be open not only to welcoming people and letting them hang out but also to welcoming people and actually inviting them to work alongside us in the essential mission of the Church. If we are not intentional about this, those of us who identify as being "the first" might just find ourselves being the last!

On the flipside of this dynamic, new parishioners might feel they have not earned the right to participate and so do not get involved with the life and work of the community beyond a surface level. I would like to remind such parishioners of the landowner in the Gospel parable, who hired the workers at the end of the day, saying, "You too go into my vineyard" (Matthew 20:7). I believe the Lord is saying

"

The Church is a living organism.

If it doesn't receive new people,

if it doesn't have new blood,

it will cease to be healthy.

to these new parishioners, "Come and work in my vineyard. It's not too late. In fact, I will pay you first, and you shall receive the same as those who have labored all day."

I think the Lord is saying to all of us, even to parishioners whose experience of Church has largely been coming to Mass and then leaving without getting involved, that the hour is late and the need is great. The Lord is inviting all of us to step beyond hanging around and come and work in the vineyard. This invitation is for everyone in every time.

When I think of how God inspires and empowers his people to go into the vineyard, I think of a woman named Flavia. I met Flavia and her family when I was pastor at Saint Benedict Parish. There we used a tool called Alpha to introduce parishioners and new people to the Christian life. (See chapter 11 for more about Alpha, an eleven-week course that I highly recommend.) Flavia had a conversion on our very first Alpha, and she went on to be our champion inviter, literally bringing hundreds of people to the course over the years.

Flavia and her husband, Jeevan, came to see me one day. They told me that they felt called by God to take Alpha into our local prison. And they did. Over four or five years, they led teams of Saint Benedict parishioners to facilitate Alpha experiences with male and female prisoners. Jeevan also became involved in a men's group in our parish and led a Bible study at his workplace.

Flavia's youngest son, Mark, also experienced a conversion, and he went on to start a ministry to the homeless. He would go out with other parishioners and colleagues from his university. They called their ministry "Greater Love." It eventually spread to other cities across Canada.

To be honest, I could not remember a time at Saint Benedict when Flavia was not actively involved in the life of the parish. It was only after knowing her a few years that I learned how much the Lord had transformed her life through a powerful experience of the Holy Spirit during her first Alpha retreat. Previously her Catholic faith had been dead: she had no personal relationship with Jesus, and the practice of her faith was only about obligation and duty. She told me that, for most of her adult life, she sat in the back row of the churches she attended and left as soon as was possible.

Not only did Flavia impact the lives of many people, but the men and women she invited to Alpha experienced conversion and would go on to impact countless others. Flavia may have entered the vineyard late in the day, but she has been paid a full-day's wage!

Finally, I'd like to reach out to those in parishes who have borne the heat of the day, who have worked hard, who were in their parishes first. Thank you for your faithfulness, for your sacrifice, and for your hard work. Your parishes would not have survived this long without your efforts on behalf of the Lord.

I would also ask you to look inside yourself to see if you can detect any unhealthy attitudes of seniority or exclusivity. Ask the Lord to shine his light on such attitudes and help you surrender them to him. Together let us not only celebrate the presence of new parishioners but also invite them to walk and serve alongside us, as we all work to bring the evangelizing mission of the Church to life in our cities, towns, and villages.

Questions for Reflection and Discussion

1. Prayerfully read through the key Scripture passages for this chapter. What words, phrases, or images catch your attention or draw your focus? What might the Lord be communicating to you through these?

2. How might you describe the difference between fairness and justice—especially as it relates to Jesus' parable about the landowner and the workers in Matthew's Gospel?

3. Are there areas in your life where you expect to be treated as though you are "first"—areas where you expect special treatment or enjoy being recognized as important? Does that influence how you see yourself or interact with others—particularly those who are also serving in a setting where you expect special treatment?

4. The Lord has a special love for the poor, the suffering, the outcast, and those seen as "the last" in this world. Are there any places in your life where you feel like the last, where you feel unwanted and overlooked? If Jesus were standing in front of you right now, what would you ask him to do for you in regard to these feelings and situations?

5. Are you involved in the life and work of your parish? Do you remember how you got started in your particular service? Was it easy or difficult for you to feel welcomed and accepted in serving your parish?

6. Think about the men and women who make up your parish community—especially those who are not deeply involved. Consider creative ways in which you and the rest of the parish can invite these folks into a more engaged response to the life and mission of the parish.

7

Christianity
for Dummies

Key Scriptures: Ezekiel 33:7-9; Matthew 18:15-20; Romans 13:8-10; 1 John 4:10

A series of books in the 1990s occupied bookstore shelves everywhere. No matter what bookstore you entered, no matter what town that bookstore was in, you could easily spot the bright yellow and black covers and bold title font of those books. The series—*For Dummies*—spanned just about every topic imaginable, promising to make those topics easy to understand: *Computers for Dummies, Baking for Dummies, Art for Dummies,* and so on. There was even one called *Christianity for Dummies.* I remember thinking, "That's the book for me."

I considered what I'd include if I wrote a book called *Christianity for Dummies.* I decided that it would have just three chapters. I'd call chapter one "God Loves Us," chapter two, "We Love God," and chapter three, "We Love One Another."

The starting point of our faith is that God has first loved us. We hear this directly in the First Letter of John: "In this is love: not that we have loved God, but that he loved us and sent his Son as expiation for our sins" (1 John 4:10). In other words, God took the initiative; he didn't wait for us to get our act together before he decided to love us.

Furthermore, our love for God, our desire to know and love him, is a response to the One who makes himself known, to the God who reveals himself and loves us. We love God because he took the initiative to love us.

Sometimes we get that mixed up. We believe that we have to do all the right things, in all the right ways, and make sure we perform in order to meet God's expectations for us—and then he will love us. That is not the starting point. God first loves us, and if we are open to receiving his love, we will grow to love him more fully and firmly in return.

Finally, it is out of our growing love for God that we experience a growing love for the things that God loves—namely, other people. God loves us, then we love God, and then we learn to truly love other people. Jesus tied these two things together: love for God and love for one another are inseparable (see, for example, John 13:34-35).

Paul writes specifically about love in the Letter to the Romans, the third key Scripture passage for this chapter: "Owe nothing to anyone, except to love one another; for the one who loves another has fulfilled the law" (Romans 13:8). He goes on to highlight the fact that all the commandments are summed up in this commandment to love.

In the Gospel of Matthew, this chapter's second key Scripture passage, Jesus' words point to the way the early Church lived, how members dealt with one another. Jesus tells his disciples that if they have a problem with someone in the community, if they have been wronged or sinned against, they should go directly to that person and talk it through. If for some reason the individual does not listen, then they should bring another person and try again. If the person does not listen to both of them, then they should bring the matter before the whole church.

Jesus describes a community whose members hold one another accountable and engage in an intimacy of life that today might make us feel uncomfortable. This intimacy of life and mutual accountability reflect an enduring reality that holds true throughout all of Scripture. Just take another look at the first key Scripture for this chapter. The prophet Ezekiel speaks to the people of Israel, who are exiled in Babylon, and basically tells them that he is going to hold them accountable for one another's spiritual life and health.

Unfortunately, this doesn't sound like the Catholics Anonymous culture that exists in many of our contemporary parishes. We might ask for advice from a priest, deacon, or member of a religious order who happens to be on staff, but we don't expect fellow parishioners to get too involved in our spiritual life.

Becoming involved in the spiritual life of another parishioner? For most Catholics, that's "none of my business." But stop for just a moment and think about this. When we say, "That's none of my business," are we not echoing that ancient cynical question that Cain raised to God, "Am I my brother's keeper?" (Genesis 4:9).

How does the Lord answer us in his Word? "Yes, you are your brother's keeper." This kind of intimate, relational communion with one another is essential if we're going to live out the fullness of what it means to love God and love one another.

Here is the critical question we must wrestle with: how can we love one another if we don't know one another?

I've often thought about how best to define Christian community and differentiate it from mere "socializing with other people." Christian community is a network of relationships in which believers are accountable to and for one another in responding to God's call to holiness and mission.

For decades we have seen the decline of Catholic parishes—in fact, of Christian communities in general, especially in the Western world. Parishes that are slowing down the decline, and even moving toward health and growth, all have one thing in common: they intentionally build community, the kind of community that the readings for this chapter describe. In these intentional communities, people know each other, actually love each other, and feel directly responsible for one another. They hold each other accountable.

Fostering Connection

After running Alpha for several years at Saint Benedict Parish, we had a number of people who hungered for deeper community. The parish was large, and the larger a parish

"

Christian community is a network
of relationships in which believers
are accountable to and for one
another in responding to God's call
to holiness and mission.

is, the more intentional it must be about creating intimate and authentic Christian community. A system of small or mid-sized groups is essential to creating this kind of community, so that people can be truly known and loved and not have to depend on their relationship with the priest for this sense of belonging.

To accomplish this, we created Connect Groups, which are groups of twenty to thirty parishioners who meet in homes every two weeks. Each session includes food, prayer, a talk or testimony by a member, and a healthy dose of laughter. People have experienced radical belonging through these Connect Groups. They have become more spiritually open and vulnerable, because they want to grow as disciples of Jesus Christ.

At Saint Benedict Parish, we had different kinds of groups. We started one for men called the Men's GYM (God You Me). After this grew and impacted many lives, a group of women came to the parish leadership with a vision to do something similar for the women of the parish. They called it GROW (God Renews Our Women).

All the Connect Groups were lay led. The members loved and cared for one another, ministered to one another, and prayed with and for one another. This way of being Church went from something strange and weird to something that was simply… normal.

The question is, how do we get there? For many of us, our communities might be further from that reality than others. Think about attending Mass at your parish. As you look around at the assembly, how many people do you actually know, let alone love? The type of knowledge I'm asking about isn't simply the knowledge of acquaintances, a level of recognition or relationship that would, at most, elicit a nod if you encountered that person at a local shop. Rather I'm talking about intimate, relational knowledge. What are this person's joys, hopes, dreams, and struggles? What burdens do they carry, and what are the joys in their life?

We have a lot of work to do as a universal Church if we are to go on this journey of living as communities of faith. The discussions, meetings, and extensive planning we have ahead of us, as individuals and members of parishes who want to thrive, can't focus on finances, buildings, and programs. We must dive into the deeper reality of communion with one another: growing to know, love, and care for one another. These are the foundational issues we must address as parishes, so that we can become communities where we know the love of God, love him in return, and live out that love by caring for one another and the world.

Questions for Reflection and Discussion

1. Prayerfully read through the key Scripture passages for this chapter. What words, phrases, or images caught your attention or drew your focus? What might the Lord be communicating to you through them?

2. What does it mean for you that God loves you? How have you experienced the love of God in your life?

3. Is it surprising, or even shocking to you in any way, that you don't have to be perfect, have your life together, or otherwise earn the love of God in your life? Why or why not?

4. What is the single biggest challenge for you personally in regard to living out the accountable, intimate, communal fellowship discussed in this chapter? What is the single biggest challenge your parish community will face in trying to live this out?

5. Name one thing that you could start doing this week to help you more intentionally respond to the needs of others in your parish. Name one thing your parish community could do this week to build authentic Christian community.

8

Bearing the Fruit
of the Kingdom

Key Scripture: Matthew 21:33-43

When I was fourteen years old, my dad placed a notice on our fridge. Actually, it was more like a declaration: "Teenagers! Tired of being harassed by your parents? Act now, move out, get a job, and pay your own bills while you still know everything!" I still remember the rather smug look on my dad's face the day he put that up.

Reading this, I found myself in a bit of a dilemma. When I was fourteen, I really *did* know everything, but the prospect of moving out and paying my own way wasn't very appealing. This notice reminded me that in my father's house, I was but a tenant, not an owner. Despite all my complaining and my opinions, my dad drove home the point that I owned nothing; none of it was mine. From a strictly human perspective, I had no right to any of my fine opinions about how life in that house should go.

In the Gospel story for this chapter, Jesus shares the parable of the tenants, where we see a similar dynamic. The tenant farmers forget that what they have is not their own. They forget that they are mere tenants who owe rent to the master.

In the agrarian culture of those days, you didn't write a check to the landlord but rather gave him a portion of the fruit of your harvest. When the master in this story sent his servants to collect the portion of the harvest he was due, the tenants abused them, beat them up, and killed them. Not only did the tenants refuse to pay their rent; they were outraged that they were even asked to pay rent. They forgot that they were tenants and acted as if they owned the land.

Where's the Fruit?

Jesus tells this parable to the Pharisees, Sadducees, scribes, and other religious leaders of his time, and he finishes with a rather startling claim. He says that the kingdom of God will be taken away from them and given to others who will produce the fruits of the kingdom (see Matthew 21:43). In other words, Jesus tells them that because they are not producing kingdom fruit (paying the rent), they will be kicked out, and the land will go to others who will produce that fruit.

This was quite an affront to the religious leaders of Jesus' time. I wonder what the Lord would say to us, his Church, today? If we are honest with ourselves, we will realize that we too struggle to produce the fruits of the kingdom.

I think the core issue behind our struggle is the same issue the tenant farmers had: we, the Church, have forgotten that we are tenants, that we are stewards and not owners. Our problem is that we think the Church, the entire kingdom of God, is ours. We talk about "my" parish, and honestly, I hope that you do feel a sense of ownership, engagement, and connection to your parish community. However, parishes are ours not in the sense that we possess them and control them. No, parishes can rightfully be considered ours only to the degree that we belong to them.

Sometimes we act (almost unconsciously) as if we actually *own* the parish, as if everything that constitutes the parish—its buildings, campuses, ways of doing things, and ministries— ultimately exist to serve our wants, needs, convenience, and desires. We forget that parishes exist for another purpose, a purpose that is beyond us. We forget that the Lord, who has given us so much, expects "rent." He expects us to produce the fruit of the kingdom.

Despite the Lord's expectations of fruit, many of our parishes are struggling. A recent Vatican document spoke to our lack of fruitfulness, stating that the life and offerings of many parishes are characterized by "mere repetitive action that fails to have an impact upon people's concrete lives [and] remains a sterile attempt at survival, which is usually welcomed by general indifference."[2] Talk about not producing the fruit of the kingdom!

We tend to do many things as parishes that don't bear fruit, but we continue to do them because that's what we have always done. If someone suggests another course of action, our instinctive response is "That's not how we do things here." Often we are committed to these actions even though they are rooted in methodologies from a bygone era, and we know they no longer work. We know—or can sense—that our efforts are not having a substantial impact on people's lives. As the instruction from the Vatican plainly says, our efforts are "sterile."

We fail to engage in the sort of fruitful missionary activity that, through God's grace, transforms lives. And lives that have been transformed are, above all else, the measure of the kingdom's fruit: not the number of bodies who show up for an event or even for Mass but rather the lives transformed by Christ. In the end, transformed people transform parishes, and transformed parishes transform the world.

Three Fundamental Conversions

There are three fundamental conversions that characterize the lives of Christians: conversion to Christ, conversion to Christ's Church, and conversion to Christ's cause.

Conversion to Christ

This conversion involves coming to know Jesus in a personal way, entering into a deep and intimate relationship with him as a person. We no longer merely know about him, as we would a subject we study, but rather we know him directly and personally. Information about Jesus rarely leads to transformation; rather the experience of his forgiveness, love, mercy, and presence leads to radical change if we surrender to him.

"

Transformed people transform parishes, and transformed parishes transform the world.

Think about it: when we enter into loving relationship with another person, it changes our perspective. It transforms us. Just so, the Lord calls each of us into a personal relationship with him.

When I was a complaining teenager with lots of opinions, one of my complaints was about being dragged to church on Sunday. I wasn't into church at all. That changed for me when I encountered Jesus. In fact, everything changed for me when I had a conversion to Christ and entered into a personal relationship with him. That began a lifelong journey of daily surrender and new chapters, as I continue my journey toward a deeper relationship with Jesus as his follower.

Conversion to Christ's Church

This conversion isn't simply about going to church, though going to church is important. Christianity is a team sport, after all. Nevertheless, many people say, "I don't need to go to church to pray." Of course not. You don't go to church just to pray.

In fact, we don't *go* to church at all. We *are* the Church. "The Church" is a collective noun meaning "the people God has called together." We are the people of God, not the persons of God. Therefore it's a bit of an oxymoron to say that you are a Christian who doesn't go to church.

We often forget the ultimate reason for the Church. The sacraments are vitally important. This is particularly true of the Sacrament of the Eucharist. In the Church's own words, the celebration of this sacrament is "the source and summit" (the beginning and the end) of our faith.[3] But celebrating sacraments doesn't exhaust the work of the Church.

We must tread the entire ground of the Church's life and mission. Ultimately, conversion to Christ's Church is about conversion to the community of God, to God's people gathered together to celebrate the Eucharist. Yet doesn't it seem strange that we can go to church in the same building every single week for twenty years and not necessarily have one single meaningful human contact? Or that we can live in isolation even among a community that is supposed to be bonded in peace?

That's not authentic Christian community. Conversion to Christ's Church means a conversion to one another. It means entering into a loving relationship not simply with God but also with those God loves. It means loving and serving one another with humility and no longer being strangers to one another.

Conversion to Christ's Cause

Did you know that Jesus has a cause? He calls it the kingdom.

I believe we have made a mistake in our understanding of this. Indeed, atheists who have critiqued Christianity throughout history have been partially right. If we make Christianity just about what we have to do to get into heaven, then all we are doing is purchasing fire insurance. And as with everything we buy, we tend to look for the cheapest price.

Don't get me wrong; being on the path to heaven is important. But there is more to a relationship with Jesus than a reward for a life well lived. A relationship with Jesus is also about allowing the power of heaven—the justice, love, mercy, and freedom of God's kingdom—to permeate the whole earth, especially our hearts. It's about getting this world to look a bit more like heaven.

This is fundamentally the work of the Church. It's our job. Why? Because it was Jesus' mission, and he passed it on to us after his resurrection. He gave us the Holy Spirit so that we could complete his work on earth, so that we could become his hands and feet. We exist as Church to transform the world, to bring it to Christ, and our parishes are placed within specific boundaries to bring light and healing and hope to those neighborhoods.

If we choose to accept our mission, we will bear the fruit of the kingdom. I'm in. How about you?

Questions for Reflection and Discussion

1. Prayerfully read the key Scripture passage for this chapter. What words, phrases, or images caught your attention or drew your focus? What might the Lord be communicating to you through them?

2. Have there been times in your life when you have taken things for granted—perhaps material objects, relationships, or even persons? How did you discover that you were doing so?

3. Have there been times in your life when you felt as if you'd taken God and his mercy, justice, love, and forgiveness for granted? What did you do when you discovered you were doing so?

4. Do you ever express an ownership over your parish, or parts of your parish life, that reflects the attitude of the tenants in Jesus' parable? If so, where do you see this? Have you seen that attitude anywhere in your parish community?

5. Where do you think you are in relation to the three conversions? Which, if any, have you experienced in your life? What might be keeping you from experiencing any of them?

9

Identity and Mission

Key Scriptures: Isaiah 55:1-2; Luke 3:15-21; 1 John 5:1-9

On October 4, 2019, my father passed away.

Recently I browsed through some photographs on my phone and came across a picture of my father from twenty years ago. I had taken it at a birthday party I threw for him. The photograph now stopped me in my tracks because of the way my father was looking at me. It was a look I would catch on his face every so often—a look that reminded me of the times he would tell me that he loved me and was proud of me. When I saw that look or heard those words, I knew that I was his beloved son and that he was pleased with me.

A great deal of ink has been spilled over the years on the importance of experiencing the love of our father and mother. From a psychological perspective, when we don't experience love from our dad and mom, we can develop real and debilitating emotional deficits. Knowing that our parents love us and hearing their pride and pleasure in us are essential, foundational experiences for us as human beings. I believe that this is infinitely truer regarding our experience of our heavenly Father's love.

In the Gospel story of the baptism of the Lord, Jesus hears his heavenly Father speak those crucial words of love and pride: "You are my beloved Son; with you I am well pleased" (Luke 3:22). In the Church's liturgical life, the Feast of the Baptism of the Lord marks a transition from the season of Christmas to the season of Ordinary Time. Scripturally this event marks a transition from the hidden life of Jesus, his first thirty years, to his public life, ministry, and mission. His baptism made his identity as the beloved Son of the Father explicit, so that he could begin to bear fruit in public ministry.

Jesus' baptism establishes a key principle for us as well: namely, that who we are is the foundation of what we do. Why is this important for us? Because as with Jesus, our identity fundamentally influences and informs what we do—our mission. If we want to intentionally live our mission as individuals and as parishes, then we must return to a sure and conscious recognition of our deepest identity as beloved children of God.

Our Baptism establishes that foundational identity. This Baptism, of course, is fundamentally different from Jesus' baptism. Jesus experienced the baptism of John, a baptism of repentance, as a symbol of his being one with sinners. We, however, bearing the stain of sin, receive the sacrament instituted by Christ that frees us from sin and makes us a participant in the life of God himself.

The word *baptism* in Greek literally means being "plunged" or "immersed." At our Baptism, we take on a new identity, because we are immersed into the person of Jesus Christ—his life, death, resurrection, and ascension. St. Paul says that when we were baptized, we went into the tomb with Jesus so that we can rise from the tomb with Jesus (see Romans 6:3-4).

At our Baptism, we were also filled with the holy Spirit. John the Baptist says this in one of the key Scripture passages for this chapter: "I am baptizing you with water, but one mightier than I is coming. I am not worthy to loosen the thongs of his sandals. He will baptize you with the holy Spirit and fire" (Luke 3:16). Think about that: God has breathed his very life into us. We are in Christ, and he is in us.

To be baptized, therefore, means to be set apart for Christ's mission. Just as Jesus began his public ministry with his baptism, we have been commissioned with Jesus at our own Baptism to give our lives for the sake of the world.

Finally, all of this is grace; all of it is pure gift. This salvation, this life into which we have been immersed, this life that God pours into us, is something we could never merit or achieve on our own. That is what the prophet Isaiah proclaims in the first key Scripture for this chapter. God calls each person to drink deeply of his life, a life that satisfies our deepest hungers and desires. Isaiah is clear, however, that we don't have to bring money or pay for it at all. It's free!

We have been baptized into Christ. As the Father looked at Jesus and saw his beloved Son, so he looks at each one of us and sees his beloved son or daughter. The Father is actually well pleased with us too—not because of our actions

"

The Father is well pleased with us—

not because of our actions or ability to

follow the rules but simply because of

who we are as baptized in Christ.

or ability to follow the rules but simply because of who we are as baptized in Christ. That is our starting point. If our starting point is anything other than the gaze of the Father, evoking a response in love, then we will experience the demands of the Christian life as burdens to be negotiated.

Scripture clearly tells us that this familial relationship with the Father, rooted in love, opens the depths of his commandments to us. Because God has loved us and we love him, we trust that God wills our deepest freedom. We know that he has given us his commandments so that, by following them, we will grow in freedom and holiness. We demonstrate our love of God by keeping them and by seeking his forgiveness when we fail to keep them.

We don't try to wriggle out of the commandments or find ways to do the bare minimum, hoping to squeak into purgatory. Rather we view the commandments as a gift of love from our heavenly Father, and we embrace them as an act of love toward him. St. John tells us that "the love of God is this, that we keep his commandments. And his commandments are not burdensome" (1 John 5:3). Knowing who we are, and *whose* we are, frees us from a "performance mentality" that sees salvation as being entirely dependent on our activity.

Without this experiential understanding of our baptismal identity, Catholics can view the Christian life as a weighty set of obligations that God has dropped on us. We can think that we have to muscle our way through by sheer force of will. Our future, given this worldview, is dependent entirely on our ability to fulfill our end of the contract.

Now, a contract is a useful legal document, but it doesn't apply at all to our relationship with God.

Covenant versus Contract

We need to recognize that we are in a *covenant* relationship with God. In Jewish tradition, a covenant is more than a legal agreement or an oath. Rather it is an exchange of persons, a mutual giving of self, with all the care and tenderness that implies.

A contract, on the other hand, is a business-oriented arrangement ensuring legal protection for each member of each contracting party. A contract represents negotiated mutual self-interest. We need contracts, of course, but if we approach our faith from a contractual perspective, we are going to experience the demands of the Gospel as a burden. Our mindset will be: how can we negotiate the best deal?

But God has joined us to himself through a covenant love. He literally laid down his life for us, and there is nothing to negotiate. We are free to enjoy a deeply personal relationship with him, confident that this covenant of love will never be broken.

We are at a turning point in the history of our Church, for sure. We have spent years wrestling with declining parishes and rampant secularization. On top of that, for the past few years we've had to cope with a pandemic that has left people feeling further isolated, cut off not only from one another but also from their parish communities. It's been tough for me, as a pastor, to walk with people on their journey of faith and not even be able to see their faces.

Yet I am convinced of this truth: we have a future! I have no idea what it's going to look like, but I do know that if we want to live in that future, we cannot cling to the past or try to renegotiate the "contracts" of the past. We need to tear up those contracts and rediscover the covenant that God has established: the covenant founded on the fact that we are his beloved sons and daughters.

When we do this, God will empower the work and prayers of his people, and we can embrace the mission for which we have been created.

Questions for Reflection and Discussion

1. Prayerfully read through the key Scripture passages for this chapter. What words, phrases, or images caught your attention or drew your focus? What might the Lord be communicating to you through them?

2. What does it mean to you that you are a beloved son or daughter of God? Is it easy for you to accept love and affirmation? Why or why not?

3. Take stock of your relationship with God. Is your starting point a covenant or a contract? Is there anything that keeps you from receiving more of the Father's love and mercy?

4. Do you ever see aspects of your parish life through the lens of a contract? How might God be asking you, as an individual, to see your parish life through the lens of covenant?

5. Is God asking you, as his son or daughter, to participate more fully in his mission? In what ways? How might God be asking your parish to participate more fully in his mission?

10

Us versus Them

Growing up in Scotland, I learned at a young age that there are two kinds of people in this world: Scots and those who wish they were Scots!

I'm sure we all have our own version of this saying; we just fill in the blank of our particular tribe. Human beings are essentially tribal: we have an affinity for our own family members, relatives, and people who are like us. This is a natural and even biological impulse, and it is not necessarily a bad one—if properly understood.

A quick look at human history, however, reveals that too often this natural affinity for like-minded people gives rise to the instinct to see the world from an "us" versus "them" perspective. This can lead to heartbreak, violence, and bloodshed.

Scripture reveals that not all exclusivity is negative, nor does it need to lead to negative tribalism. The exclusivity of the Jewish nation as the chosen people of God, for example, led directly to the inclusion of all people through the sacrifice of Jesus. The key Scriptures for this chapter make this clear.

In the first reading, the prophet talks about the Temple, a uniquely Jewish institution, and he says something remarkable. In the future, the "foreigners who join themselves to the LORD," the Gentiles, will come into the Temple joyfully and lay their sacrifices at the altar. The Lord declares that his house will be "a house of prayer for all peoples" (Isaiah 56:6-7).

This was a slowly unfolding process, however. In the reading from Matthew, we see Jesus with a Gentile, a Canaanite woman, in an unusual interaction focused on inclusion and exclusion. The woman wants Jesus to free her daughter from a demon, but he tells her that's not his job: he was sent only to "the lost sheep of the house of Israel" (Matthew 15:24). The woman persists, even as Jesus goes on to compare Canaanites to dogs, who are not to take food from the children. Ultimately Jesus rather admiringly grants her request: "O woman, great is your faith! Let it be done for you as you wish" (15:28).

Paul develops this theme more intensely in his Letter to the Romans. God chose the Jewish people to reveal the light of salvation to the world. Such was the importance of his Chosen People that he would use even their failure to bring about the salvation of the world in Christ Jesus (see Romans 11:11).

All of salvation history hangs upon this truth: out of love for his people, God bound himself to Israel and made an exclusive covenant with that nation, saying to them, you are a people fully my own; you are a holy and chosen people. From this high point of exclusivity, God brought about the greatest act of inclusivity: the life, death, resurrection, and ascension of Jesus, who opened salvation to *all* people, Jew and Gentile alike.

Our culture highly values inclusivity and devalues exclusivity. But Scripture reveals that there can be a positive connection between the two. What does this mean for us as a Church? Through the exclusive covenant God made with Israel and the inclusive sacrificial action of Jesus, God has brought salvation for all peoples.

Lourdes

After my second year of theological studies in the seminary, I did the student thing and spent three weeks backpacking through Europe. After visiting Paris, I took the train south to Lourdes. I arrived in Lourdes, and I found my hotel at around three p.m. Since my room was not ready, I left my bags at the desk and went for a walk, eventually heading toward the main shrine.

The closer I got to the church, the more crowded the streets became. Gift shops and hawkers of cheap and cheesy religious baubles were seemingly everywhere. I had anticipated that this visit would be a sublime spiritual experience. Instead I felt as if I had entered the Temple precincts to become lost amid the money changers' tables. I was angry and more than a little turned off by the jostling crowds, the aggressive restauranteurs, and the innumerable religious plastic statues. I was done with Lourdes. What a waste of time, I thought to myself.

Suddenly the crowd parted, and I saw the basilica. A procession of hundreds was coming toward me. The people were praying the Rosary, and at the end of each decade, they sang the Song of Lourdes. Voices from across the globe joined in the Latin chorus: "Ave, Ave, Ave Maria."

I had been raised with a homogenous experience of Church, in Scotland and in Canada. Now I saw men and women of every tribe and nation, of every race and tongue, united together in a common faith. Young and old, able-bodied and physically challenged, walked toward me. I experienced something profound in that moment: a sure and certain knowledge that this is what it meant for the Church to be catholic My self-righteous anger melted away, and I began to weep. With tears running down my face, I croaked out, "Ave, Ave, Ave Maria."

Our Church is not defined by any particular nationality, ethnicity, race, or language. It is for all peoples. This Church carries an inclusive message rooted in an exclusive claim: that Jesus Christ is Savior, and Christians receive his life and become sons and daughters of God.

We have to embrace our exclusive identity as Christians, or we will never be able to live out our inclusive mission. If we do not believe that we are God's children—that he has chosen us uniquely and gifted us to be channels of his love—then we will never be able to bear fruit by sharing the universal message of salvation.

"

We have to embrace our

exclusive identity as Christians,

or we will never be able to live

out our inclusive mission.

The Lord wants all people to come joyfully to his house—his Church. He wants people from every race, tribe, and tongue to lay their sacrifices down at his altar. He wants everyone to know that the Lord's house is a house of prayer for the whole world.

Will we answer his call?

Questions for Reflection and Discussion

1. What "tribes"—family, friends, school, parish, and so forth—are you part of? How do you determine who is inside each tribe versus who is outside? What is the general attitude of these tribes toward those who are outside?

2. How do you experience your membership in your parish? Do you experience it in the universal sense, as part of the larger communion of the Church? Or do you experience yourself primarily as a member of a local group of people who have worshipped together for years, served together in ministries, and live in the same parts of town?

3. What is the message of salvation that Jesus brings? What must we do to receive that gift? How have you responded personally to that message? How have you helped people encounter the reality of that message? How is your parish helping others encounter that message?

4. What do strangers and newcomers to your parish experience when they come onto your campus? What kind of welcome might they receive? What processes do you have to help guests and potential new families feel connected and welcomed?

11

Catching Fish

Key Scripture: Mark 1:14-20

Over the last ten years, I have made five trips to the Holy Land, four of which were pilgrimages that I had the great blessing to lead. The Holy Land offers many wonderful sites and opportunities for reflection. My absolute favorite place to visit is the Sea of Galilee.

I love the Sea of Galilee because of its permanence. In Jerusalem much has changed over two thousand years, but at the Sea of Galilee, I can take in the same things that Jesus did. I look at the mountains and the skyline that he gazed upon, and I take in the same sounds of birds and the same smell of pollen carried by the sea breeze. The sea may have shrunk a bit since the time of Jesus, but it is still there. You could even say that when you are at the Sea of Galilee, you may be walking on some of the same stones that Jesus did.

I absolutely love being there!

On these pilgrimages, I take our travelers around the Sea of Galilee to Capernaum and to Bethsaida, where Peter, Andrew, and Philip were from (see John 1:44). Eventually we make our way to the west side of the sea, where we have lunch at a kibbutz that hosts a big outdoor restaurant with large tents. They serve something there called St. Peter's fish.

The first time I visited, I was excited to order this item. But when they put the meal in front of me—with the head still attached—I was more than a little put off. I'd never had my lunch stare balefully at me in quite the same way as that St. Peter's fish did. Honestly, I kind of lost my appetite.

But if this sea was the water Jesus walked on, and these mountains the ones he looked upon, this was definitely the fish he ate. So I tucked in and discovered I was eating a delicious tilapia. And I ate until only the bones remained.

The key Scripture for this chapter, from the Gospel of Mark, speaks about the call of Peter, Andrew, James, and John. It also talks about fishing nets, catching fish, and catching people. Now, catching people should concern us most of all, as it is the fundamental mission of the Church.

Mission!

Jesus uses three dominant images for the mission of the Church: the image of fishing, the image of feeding lambs and sheep, and the image of reaping the harvest. We find these three metaphors throughout the whole of the New Testament, but two of them—catching fish and feeding sheep or lambs—have dominated the Church's vision of her activity over the last millennia. And feeding sheep or shepherding has become the default image of the Church's understanding of ministry and leadership. The image of Jesus as shepherd, the role of priests as shepherds, and the fact that ministry is a shepherding activity: these have been the primary way the Church has understood herself and her role in the world.

As I've said, I am the pastor of Our Lady of Guadalupe Parish. In Latin my title, "pastor," merely means "shepherd." I am a shepherd to my people. The bishop never appointed me fisherman, nor am I called Farmer James. My primary role, and the role of those who collaborate with me, is the pastoral care—the shepherding—of the people of God.

We don't speak about spiritual combine harvesters or fishing fleets when describing the Church's activity. We have given shepherding the privileged place in our common understanding of the role of pastoral ministry. But we used to speak more frequently of fishing. If we really want to have a full picture of the Church's life and mission, I would say that it must both fish and shepherd.

Yes, we are called to care for the sheep that we have. That is part of my official role as pastor and also a responsibility of the whole people of God. We must be caring, loving, supportive communities of faith. We can't just depend on priests, deacons, and staff to make that happen in our parishes. We have to own this responsibility together if we want to become a Church that cares for sheep, feeds them, and helps them grow. In one sense, I would call this "maintenance." We maintain the flock of God.

However, Jesus also sends us on a mission: he says to "go." In fact, in Luke's Gospel, he tells his disciples to "put out into deep water and lower your nets for a catch" (Luke

5:4). We are called to go to those on the outside, not just serve those on the inside. Our call is not either/or; it's both/and. We are called to fish as well as to care for the sheep.

We have a good grasp of our need to care for the sheep; I would say that today we need to learn how to fish. For two reasons.

Number one: Jesus commanded us to. Jesus told his disciples that he would make them fishers of people (see Mark 1:17; Luke 5:10). We are to be a community that catches people for Jesus. We need to learn how to do it so we can be obedient to Jesus.

The second reason we must learn how to fish is for our future. For roughly the last thousand years, we've lived in what has been, for the most part, a Christian culture. The primary model of ministry, or plan for how the Church would survive and thrive, was to minister to the sheep who showed up. When you feed the sheep who show up, they grow up, get married, and have baby sheep. Then we feed the baby sheep, and they grow up, get married, and have baby sheep—and so on.

However, in the last twenty to thirty years, 90 percent of the baby sheep have grown up and left the flock. Unfortunately, there's not much sign of their coming back. The reasons for this current reality are many and varied and largely beyond the scope of this book.

Yet the problem remains: we cannot simply rely on ministering to the sheep who show up. We must relearn what it means to be a Church that goes fishing. The question becomes "How do we do this?" This question is critical, because if we don't get the "how" right, we won't have nets that are full.

In answering this question and doing what it takes to live out the "how," we are responding to the Church's call to *evangelization*.

There's that word. Pope Paul VI wrote, "Evangelizing is in fact the grace and vocation proper to the Church, her deepest identity. She exists in order to evangelize."[4]

Let's be honest. Aren't we a lot more comfortable with feeding sheep than we are with catching fish? So how do we fish?

Perhaps some of you are thinking that the Church wants you to stand on the street corner and yell at people, force the Bible on them, or have uncomfortable conversations in coffee shops. No. That is not what the Church proposes.

I have wrestled with the how of evangelization for most of my adult life and certainly throughout my priesthood. As I've said, as a teenager, I didn't like church. I found it boring and irrelevant. But then I encountered Jesus in a way that changed my life. I was caught for Jesus. From that time on, I wanted parishes to become places where Jesus could catch people, not simply places where we cared for sheep. I wanted churches to be fishing boats. I wanted parishioners to be fishermen and fisherwomen, casting their nets wide to catch those Jesus was calling to himself.

If we look at our parishes today and somehow convince ourselves that they are fishing boats, we have to conclude that they are mostly tied up at the dock. Most parishes that manage to catch fish do so because the fish swim into the

"

Alpha is primarily a tool to catch fish. It focuses on building relationships and on the basic proclamation of the gospel.

harbor and jump into the boat. There is not a lot of intentional fishing going on.

The Alpha Tool

As I have wrestled with the how of evangelization throughout the years, I have discovered a tool that works—one that is so effective that if you use it well, it will transform an entire parish. I have seen this happen multiple times. That tool's name is Alpha.

Some of you may have heard about Alpha, while for others it sounds new. Some of you may be positively disposed toward this tool, while some of you may not be. There are many tools you can use to help you learn to catch fish, but I believe that the Alpha process is the most effective.

Alpha consists of ten weekly sessions that are specifically geared toward those who are far from Christ and his Church. Alpha can definitely feed the sheep, but it is primarily a tool to catch fish. The Alpha process uses a welcoming, nonjudgmental dynamic to foster conversation about the big questions in life. It creates a space where people can come to know one another by sharing a meal, watching a video or listening to a live talk, and then discussing it. The heart of Alpha is dialogue, not teaching. Alpha focuses on building relationships and on the basic proclamation of the gospel.

Our Catholic faith is very rich; we have a lot of history and tradition. As wonderful as that is, the downside of it is that we tend to clutter things up and overwhelm folks who are not ready to digest the rich food of our Tradition.

Alpha begins with the simple things. Later we can build on those simple things.

One of the strengths of Alpha as a tool lies in the fact that it is communal evangelization. Think of fishing: you can fish with either a net or a fishing rod. If you are fishing in a small river, you might choose a rod over a net. However, when you are out in the deep, where the fish are plentiful, it is more effective to have several people work together using a net.

In Alpha we each step in, bringing our own gifts and skills to the task. Communal evangelization equals teamwork. And when we work together, evangelization is not only more fun but also less threatening.

Jumping to It

In Mark's Gospel, we read that after Jesus' invitation, the disciples abandoned their nets and immediately followed him. *Immediately.*

That word "immediately" appears twice in this key Scripture passage. It is one of Mark's favorite words. It speaks to us of the urgency of the task—the task to be a Church that fishes for people. Why is this urgent?

Because Jesus calls us to it. Jesus says, follow me, and I will make you fishers of people. If you don't feel equipped right now, that's perfectly fine. Jesus says, *I will make* you a fisher of people. Jesus will teach us the way. All of the other priorities we have as dioceses and parishes must be seen in light of this urgent call to evangelize.

Why? Because evangelization is about the heart, and when you transform the heart, everything else flows from that.

Catching fish may not be as comfortable for you as tending sheep. Some of you might be excited about the prospect, but many of you are probably feeling the way I felt when that St. Peter's fish glared at me from my lunch plate. But I want to invite you, as individuals and as parishes, to "taste and see."

It may not look appealing, but trust me: it's delicious!

Questions for Reflection and Discussion

1. Prayerfully read through the key Scripture passage for this chapter. What words, phrases, or images caught your attention or drew your focus? What might the Lord be communicating to you through them?

2. What images does the word "evangelization" evoke for you?

3. Have you had experience as an individual "fisher of people" for Jesus? How successful were your efforts? What did you learn along the way?

4. Does your parish have a particular tool that it uses to evangelize? Have you been part of that process? What was it like? What effect is that process having on individuals and on your community?

12

Rejoice Always!

Since I was ordained as a deacon, I have probably officiated at close to five hundred weddings. Perhaps my favorite moment of the Rite of Holy Matrimony is the exchange of vows.

This ought to be everyone's favorite moment actually, because it is the moment when the sacrament actually takes place. I ask the bride and groom to stand in the center of the sanctuary, in front of the altar, and turn to face one another. Then I get out of the way—because the deacon or priest at a wedding is simply the witness—and the couple speak their vows to one another.

The moment of exchanging vows is the most joyful part of the rite. After it I invite the newly married couple to give each other a kiss, and everyone applauds. Some people believe that you are not married until the ring is on the finger, but the marriage begins at the exchange of vows.

I presided at one wedding more than ten years ago that unfolded in the usual manner: the couple exchanged vows and kissed, and everyone applauded. It was a joyful moment, perhaps the most joyful moment the newly married couple had experienced in their young lives. Then, when the applause stopped, a man in the fourth pew suddenly stood up.

Everyone turned to look at the man as he stepped into the aisle. He took two steps toward the back of the church and collapsed, groaning as he hit the floor. The whole church gasped and then froze. Five seconds after a moment of intense happiness, we were all experiencing intense anxiety and alarm.

The good news in all this is that the married couple were newly minted doctors, and there were about fifty doctors in the church for the wedding. Within seconds the man was attentively cared for. The paramedics arrived to take him to the hospital, and all turned out well for the man, who I later learned was the bride's uncle.

I have never forgotten that experience of moving from happiness to the exact opposite within such a short span of time. It was as if someone had turned off the light. I suspect that many of us have had an experience like this. We went from being extremely happy to having that happiness suddenly disappear. Those times reinforce the reality that happiness is fragile and so very vulnerable to circumstances.

For this reason, I want to make a distinction between happiness and joy.

God Is Good—All the Time!

Happiness depends a great deal on our immediate circumstances and on our emotions—both of which can change quite dramatically and swiftly. Joy, however, consists of something deeper and more substantial. Joy is grounded in the supernatural life of God. It therefore transcends our circumstances and emotions.

The Church understands this deeply. The season of Advent is a time of preparation and repentance. In the middle of that season, we celebrate Gaudete Sunday. The word *Gaudete* is Latin for "rejoice." We are called to rejoice in the midst of our repentance, to rejoice in the midst of our waiting. We hear that call in many of our Advent hymns. And the rose-colored candle in the Advent wreath during that third week reminds us to rejoice.

The theme of rejoicing runs through the key Scriptures for this chapter. In Paul's First Letter to the Thessalonians, he instructs the Church: "Rejoice always. Pray without ceasing. In all circumstances give thanks, for this is the will of God for you in Christ Jesus" (1 Thessalonians 5:16-18).

Rejoice always, in *all* circumstances.

Many of you might be thinking, "Is that even possible?" The answer is "Yes. It is!"

I don't think it's possible to be *happy* in all circumstances. To be honest, when I meet people who seem to be happy all the time, they get on my nerves. There is something weird and disingenuous about it—as if they are programmed androids. I do believe, however, that it's possible to be *joyful* all the time—even in the midst of the challenging circumstances of life, in times of suffering, hardship, grief, or confusion. We can even be joyful when we find ourselves dealing with a pandemic, during which all these things might be happening at the same time.

This is not simply a theological conviction. I have experienced it. In the not-too-distant past, circumstances beyond my control created a situation that was very difficult and quite frightening. During some moments of that extended ordeal, I was paralyzed with fear and anxiety. It was one of the most difficult experiences of my life. And yet at a particular stretch of time in the middle of that situation, I experienced the most intense joy I've ever had.

I remember thinking that this made no sense. Why was I so joyful when I found myself in such a rotten situation? There really was no explanation. In reflecting further on it, I discovered that my joy came from this single fact: no matter what happened, nothing would change the truth that I'm a son of God, that God is my Father, and that in spite of my brokenness, my weaknesses, and my sins, I'm loved by my Father. God's mercy is like a torrential river that I can immerse myself in at any moment. Nothing changes the fact that my God loves me, no matter what.

People wonder what the key to the distinction between joy and happiness might be, and it is just this: to know the love and mercy of God, not just in our heads but experientially, in our lives. This is the key to unlocking joy in every moment of our lives.

"

To know the love and mercy
of God, not just in our heads but
experientially, in our lives. . . . This
is the key to unlocking joy in
every moment of our lives.

We hear from the prophet Isaiah in the first key Scripture for this chapter:

> I will rejoice heartily in the LORD,
>   my being exults in my God;
> For he has clothed me with garments of
>   salvation. (Isaiah 61:10)

Now Is the Time

To be wrapped in a garment is experiential, and salvation ought to be experiential as well. We often think of salvation as abstract or something that we will receive when we die. That is of course true: we will experience the fullness of salvation after our death. However, we can experience—and we ought to experience—God's salvation *in the present moment.*

St. Paul writes, "Behold, now is a very acceptable time; behold, now is the day of salvation" (2 Corinthians 6:2). Right now, in this very moment, the Lord wants to wrap us in the garment of salvation. He wants us to experience his mercy and his love.

Before we can talk about the experience of God's mercy and love, however, we need to stop and acknowledge the fact that we're making a big presumption: the presumption that God is merciful. In other words, how do we know that God wants to be merciful and fill us with his love? We know it from what he has revealed about himself in the Scriptures, of course.

One of my favorite Bible passages comes from Paul's Letter to the Romans: "But God proves his love for us in that while we were still sinners Christ died for us" (Romans 5:8). The text says that God *proves* his love for us, while other translations say that God *demonstrates* his love for us, *shows* his love for us, and *reveals* his love for us. These are all good translations, because the word from the original text carries all of these meanings.

We know that God loves us and wants us to experience his mercy and love because he gave us his son, Jesus, the Lamb of God. The Gospel passage for this chapter describes Jesus as the light of God who comes into the darkness of our world and into the darkness of our hearts (see John 1:9). The Scriptures tell us that God is the one who takes the initiative.

The First Letter of John says it plainly: "We love because he first loved us" (1 John 4:19). God did not wait for us to get our act together or to clean ourselves up; he loves us while we are still in our sins. God takes the initiative and invites us to respond. When we respond to him, through his grace, we experience his mercy and love. We experience the joy of salvation.

We find the ultimate proof that God wants us to experience his mercy and love in the cross of Jesus Christ. The coming of Jesus, his birth and his life among us, was for one purpose: that he might suffer and die on the cross for the sake of our salvation. Therefore our sins and our failings, and all the things we are not proud of in our lives, need not be obstacles to our relationship with God. In Jesus Christ, these things do not define us. And through his mercy and grace, even these obstacles can become the means through which we come to experience his salvation.

In the passage from John's Gospel, we hear about John the Baptist, one of the central figures we reflect on during the season of Advent. In all the Gospel passages in which John the Baptist appears, we see the prophet Isaiah quoted: Prepare the way! Someone is coming, and we've got to get ready. Prepare the way of the Lord (see Matthew 3:3; Mark 1:2-4; Luke 3:4-6; John 1:23).

John the Baptist sees himself as simply "the voice of one crying out in the desert" to "make straight the way of the Lord" (John 1:23; see Isaiah 40:3). For the contemporaries of John the Baptist, the desert (or the wilderness) meant the wild places of Judea that were rugged, rough, and barren. The wilderness of Judea would seem to them a pretty strange place to say, "Make straight the way of the Lord," because there aren't many straight, flat features in that wilderness. That's why we also hear about making the crooked way straight and smoothing out the rough places (see Luke 3:5).

John the Baptist says that the Lord is coming, and he is coming so that we can experience his salvation. This is the cry of the gospel message.

But we have to do our part. We have to respond to this moment in time and prepare the way of the Lord in our own life. Think about this: if you were told that a very important guest was coming to visit your house, wouldn't you clean up the yard, tidy the house, and generally remove any obstacle that would prevent this guest from entering and enjoying your home?

Prepare the Way

In the season of Advent, the Church calls us to focus on making straight the Lord's path, but the Lord's invitation to us, his desire that we receive him, occurs in every season. To make straight the way of the Lord is to prepare ourselves so that nothing will hinder the Lord from coming fully into our lives. This is not simply about celebrating the historical coming of Jesus two thousand years ago. Nor is it simply about anticipating his coming in glory at the end of time. It is also about his coming to us now, today!

Jesus wants to come to every single one of us today, so that we may experience his mercy and grace and be "clothed . . . with garments of salvation" (Isaiah 61:10). He wants to fill us with his life, so that we may know joy regardless of our circumstances.

One of the ways we prepare to receive the Lord fully, to prepare his way in our life, is to celebrate the Sacrament of Reconciliation. Pope Francis has described the sacrament in this way: "Celebrating the Sacrament of Reconciliation means being enfolded in a warm embrace."[5] This image recalls that of being wrapped in the garments of salvation. We experience the love and mercy of God as we engage in that ancient practice of confessing our sins.

When we recall our personal history, celebrating the Sacrament of Reconciliation may not have always felt like a warm embrace or an experience of mercy and grace. If this is the case for you, the prospect of Confession may not fill you with excitement. But whatever your experience has been, I want to invite you to return to that sacrament as a way of clearing out the debris that keeps you from receiving the Lord more fully. Be open to the possibility that the Lord wants to come to you in a new way.

Like Paul, I truly believe that this *is* the moment of salvation. The Lord wants you to know him in a deeper way and to experience—whether for the first time or in an intensified way—his great mercy, love, and forgiveness. God has proved his great love for you in Jesus, and now this Jesus invites you to know the joy of salvation even in the midst of the storms of life. While happiness will fade, the joy of the Lord endures.

Rejoice always!

Questions for Reflection and Discussion

1. Prayerfully read through the key Scripture passages for this chapter. What words, phrases, or images caught your attention or drew your focus? What might the Lord be communicating to you through them?

2. The distinction between joy and happiness may seem like a subtle one. If someone asked you to explain the difference between these two experiences, how would you answer?

3. Have you ever had an experience of joy in the midst of challenging times, even during a period of trial or suffering? What was that experience like? Did you specifically ask for the grace to rejoice? If not, where do you think that grace came from?

4. The idea of experiencing salvation in the present moment often bumps up against our understanding of salvation as something we receive after this life, in heaven. Thinking back on your own life, were there times when the love, mercy, and presence of God were tangible? What happened, and how did that affect you?

5. What was your earliest experience of the Sacrament of Reconciliation like? How has that influenced your approach and openness to the sacrament?

6. In addition to receiving the Sacrament of Reconciliation, what are some other ways you can "prepare the way of the Lord," that you might receive him in the "wilderness" of your heart this week?

Conclusion

Thank you, dear reader, for persevering to the end of this short book. This is a very different kind of book than the ones I have previously written. This is the first time I've written for the people in the pews and not just for pastors, clergy, and members of parish pastoral councils. It has been wonderful to journey with you and share my heart with you. I hope that whatever the Lord has provoked in your heart will be shared with other parishioners. Perhaps you may feel the call of the Lord to gather a small group of parishioners to work through the chapters of this book together and use the discussion questions as a guide. Never underestimate the power of your yes to the Lord. An authentic yes is a contagious yes—a yes that can transform an entire community.

Finally, I'll let you in on a small secret. Although each of these chapters were based on homilies that I preached to my parishioners, in truth, the first person I was preaching to was the person who needed to hear and receive the message the most. That person was me. So please pray for me and pray for my little parish, that we may never settle for surviving but constantly strive to be thriving.

Notes

1. Pope Francis, Apostolic Exhortation *Evangelii Gaudium* [The Joy of the Gospel], November 24, 2013, 49, vatican.va/content/francesco/en/apost_exhortations/documents/papa-francesco_esortazione-ap_20131124_evangelii-gaudium.html.

2. Congregation for the Clergy, "The Pastoral Conversion of the Parish Community in the Service of the Evangelising Mission of the Church," July 20, 2020, 17, https://press.vatican.va/content/salastampa/en/bollettino/pubblico/2020/07/20/200720a.html.

3. Vatican II, *Lumen Gentium* [Dogmatic Constitution on the Church], 11, in Austin Flannery, ed., *Vatican Council II: Volume 1, The Conciliar and Post Conciliar Documents,* new rev. ed. (Northport, NY: Costello, 1996), 362.

4. Pope Paul VI, Apostolic Exhortation *Evangelii Nuntiandi* [Evangelization in the Modern World], December 8, 1975, 14, https://www.vatican.va/content/paul-vi/en/apost_exhortations/documents/hf_p-vi_exh_19751208_evangelii-nuntiandi.html.

5. Pope Francis, General Audience, February 19, 2014, 3, https://www.vatican.va/content/francesco/en/audiences/2014/documents/papa-francesco_20140219_udienza-generale.html.

Divine Renovation Ministry

At Divine Renovation ministry, we come alongside leaders in their work to bring their parish or diocese on mission. Whether you're new to the journey or if you've been on it for years, our team is ready to join with you in bringing your diocese or parish from maintenance to mission. Reach out to connect, and learn more at divinerenovation.org.

www.divinerenovation.org

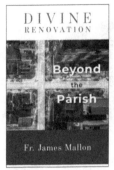

Divine Renovation Beyond the Parish

The world is hungering for the fruit of a dynamic Church that has embraced her missionary identity, but what does it really mean to be a missionary Church? Grounded in Scripture and Sacred Tradition, Fr. Mallon offers an analysis of the challenges the Church is facing, along with practical tools that will support parish and diocesan leaders in bringing about significant renewal. Most importantly, he addresses the critical interface between a missionary parish and its diocese, essential to bearing lasting fruit.

Product Code: BDRDE9

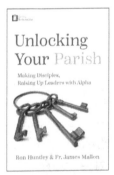

Unlocking Your Parish

Can Catholic parishes become communities of missionary disciples that bear lasting fruit? If so, what does it take to move them in that direction?

Through his years as pastor of Saint Benedict Parish in Halifax, Canada, Fr. James Mallon discovered that the answer to the first question was a resounding yes! Tailored for Catholics, Alpha played a key role in the transformation of the parish he pastored.

Unlocking Your Parish: Making Disciples, Raising Up Leaders with Alpha aims to provide insight into what Alpha can do to help any Catholic parish become a vibrant, mission-focused community.

Product Code: BDRCE8

Fr. Simon Lobo, CC

Divine Renovation Apprentice

Transforming a parish is challenging, demanding, and sometimes messy work. Divine Renovation Apprentice, Fr. Simon Lobo breaks open his experience as an associate pastor working on the renewal of Saint Benedict Parish in Halifax, Nova Scotia, the birthplace of Divine Renovation. With honesty, humility, and great clarity, Fr. Simon offers his personal reflections on the actual process of renovation with practical wisdom critical to anyone who wants to see their parish experience new life. More than simply a biographical account of the change at Saint Benedict, this book contains insights on how to change culture, build a game plan, and develop leaders for lasting parish change.
Product Code: BDRBE8

To order, visit bookstore.wau.org or call 1-800-775-9673.

the WORD
among us®
The *Spirit* of Catholic Living

This book was published by The Word Among Us. Since 1981, The Word Among Us has been answering the call of the Second Vatican Council to help Catholic laypeople encounter Christ in the Scriptures.

The name of our company comes from the prologue to the Gospel of John and reflects the vision and purpose of all of our publications: to be an instrument of the Spirit, whose desire is to manifest Jesus' presence in and to the children of God. In this way, we hope to contribute to the Church's ongoing mission of proclaiming the gospel to the world so that all people would know the love and mercy of our Lord and grow more deeply in their faith as missionary disciples.

Our monthly devotional magazine, *The Word Among Us*, features meditations on the daily and Sunday Mass readings, and currently reaches more than one million Catholics in North America and another half million Catholics in one hundred countries around the world. Our book division, The Word Among Us Press, publishes numerous books, Bible studies, and pamphlets that help Catholics grow in their faith.

To learn more about who we are and what we publish, log on to our website at www.wau.org. There you will find a variety of Catholic resources that will help you grow in your faith.

Embrace His Word, Listen to God . . .

www.wau.org